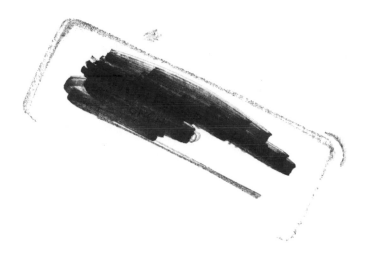

394

COUNTRIES OF THE WORLD

Ethiopia

Gareth Stevens Publishing
A WORLD ALMANAC EDUCATION GROUP COMPANY

About the Author: Elizabeth Berg lives and works in the United States. She has extensive experience as a freelance writer and has written and edited many children's books.

Written by
ELIZABETH BERG

Edited by
KEN CHANG

Designed by
HASNAH MOHD ESA

Picture research by
SUSAN JANE MANUEL

Updated and reprinted in 2005.
First published in North America in 2000 by
Gareth Stevens Publishing
A World Almanac Education Group Company
330 West Olive Street, Suite 100
Milwaukee, Wisconsin 53212 USA

Please visit our web site at
www.garethstevens.com
For a free color catalog describing
Gareth Stevens Publishing's list of
high-quality books and multimedia programs,
call 1-800-542-2595 (USA) or 1-800-387-3178 (Canada).
Gareth Stevens Publishing's fax: (414) 332-3567.

© **TIMES MEDIA PRIVATE LIMITED 2000**
© **MARSHALL CAVENDISH INT'L (ASIA) PTE LTD 2004**
Originated and designed by Times Editions
An imprint of Marshall Cavendish International (Asia) Pte Ltd
A member of the Times Publishing Group
Times Centre, 1 New Industrial Road
Singapore 536196
http://www.timesone.com.sg/te

Library of Congress Cataloging-in-Publication Data
Berg, Elizabeth, 1953–
Ethiopia / by Elizabeth Berg.
p. cm. -- (Countries of the world)
Includes bibliographical references and index.
Summary: An introduction to the geography, history, government, lifestyles, culture, and current issues of Ethiopia.
ISBN 0-8368-2324-9 (lib. bdg.)
1. Ethiopia--Juvenile literature. [1. Ethiopia.] I. Title.
II. Countries of the world (Milwaukee, Wis.)
DT373.B47   2000
963--dc21   00-020205

Printed in Singapore

3 4 5 6 7 8 9 09 08 07 06 05 04

PICTURE CREDITS
Archive Photos: 82
Michele Burgess: 2, 5, 20, 22, 28, 31 (bottom), 35, 51, 59 (top), 65, 70 (bottom), 85
Camerapix: cover, 3 (top), 3 (center), 7, 10, 12, 14, 15 (bottom), 21 (top), 31 (top), 32, 33 (bottom), 37, 41, 43, 48, 49, 52, 54, 57, 60, 64, 68, 69, 77, 78, 80
Ann Cook/MEP: 19, 70 (top), 87
Teri Gentry: 83
HBL Network Photo Agency: 56
Hutchison Library: 8, 34, 40, 58, 61, 63
Bjorn Klingwall: 4, 16, 17, 18, 27, 29, 33 (top), 36, 53, 55, 67, 71, 89
North Wind Picture Archives: 11
Christine Osborne/MEP: 79
Paul Rozario: 90
Liba Taylor: 24, 42, 66
Topham Picturepoint: 1, 3 (bottom), 6, 9, 13 (both), 15 (top), 15 (center), 21 (bottom), 23, 25, 26, 30, 38, 39, 46, 47, 62, 72, 73, 74, 75, 76, 81 (both), 84, 91
Trip Photographic Library: 59 (bottom)
Vision Photo Agency/Hulton Getty: 44, 45, 50

Digital Scanning by Superskill Graphics Pte Ltd

Contents

HARRIET TUBMAN

(Born 1822 • Died 1913)

c. 1868

c. 1875

Araminta "Minty" Ross was born into slavery on a plantation in
Maryland. A slave is someone who is owned by another person
and is forced to work for them without being paid. Slavery was
legal in America when Minty was born. The first slave in Minty's
family was her grandmother who was taken from her home in
Africa and brought to America on a ship. She was enslaved by
white owners. Minty's family, along with many others, worked on
plantations—places where crops were grown. Minty was forced to
work from the age of five. But she had a fighting spirit and always
stood up for herself and others. One day, a man hit her on the
head while she was trying to help a runaway slave. The injury was

c. 1885   2009

so bad that she was in pain for the rest of her life. In 1849, Minty made a plan to escape. She changed her name to Harriet Tubman and made a dangerous journey north to the states where slavery no longer existed. Once she was free, she went back for others. The skills she picked up on these missions helped her during the Civil War. She led an operation to free hundreds of slaves, crippling the plantation where they worked. In her later years, Harriet spoke up about women's rights and helped the people she had freed to start new lives, as laws were still unequal for African Americans. Harriet sacrificed so much throughout her life to help others. She is a symbol of strength, hope, and bravery for many people around the world.

Want to find out more about **Harriet Tubman?**
Read one of these great books:

Minty: A Story of Young Harriet Tubman by Alan Schroeder and Jerry Pinkney
Who Was Harriet Tubman? by Yona Zeldis McDonough and Nancy Harrison
I Am Harriet Tubman by Brad Meltzer and Christopher Eliopoulos

If you're in Maryland, you could even visit the Harriet Tubman Underground Railroad State Park to learn more about her life.

Brimming with creative inspiration, how-to projects, and useful information to enrich your everyday life, Quarto Knows is a favorite destination for those pursuing their interests and passions. Visit our site and dig deeper with our books into your area of interest: Quarto Creates, Quarto Cooks, Quarto Homes, Quarto Lives, Quarto Drives, Quarto Explores, Quarto Gifts, or Quarto Kids.

Text © 2018 Mª Isabel Sánchez Vegara. Illustrations © 2018 Pili Aguado.

First published in the UK in 2018 by Lincoln Children's Books, an imprint of The Quarto Group.
400 First Avenue North, Suite 400, Minneapolis, MN 55401, USA.
T (612) 344-8100 F (612) 344-8692 **www.QuartoKnows.com**
First published in Spain in 2018 under the title Pequeña & Grande Harriet Tubman
by Alba Editorial, s.l.u., Baixada de Sant Miquel, 1, 08002 Barcelona
www.albaeditorial.es

A catalog record for this book is available from the British Library.
ISBN 978-1-78603-227-0

The illustrations were created with ink, markers, and digital techniques. Set in Futura BT

Published by Rachel Williams • Designed by Karissa Santos
Edited by Katy Flint • Production by Jenny Cundill

Manufactured in Guangdong, China CC072018

9 8 7 6 5 4 3 2

Photographic acknowledgments (pages 28-29, from left to right) 1. Harriet Tubman, 1868–1869 from the Collection of the Smithsonian National Museum of African American History and Culture shared with the Library of Congress. 2. Harriet Tubman, 1860–1875 © copyright Alpha Historica / Alamy Stock Photo. 3. Harriet Tubman, 1885 © copyright GL Archive / Alamy Stock Photo. 4. Harriet Tubman Monument in Boston Massachusetts, 2009 © copyright Anthony Pleva / Alamy Stock Photo.

Also in the *Little People*, **BIG DREAMS** series:

FRIDA KAHLO

ISBN: 978-1-84780-783-0

Meet Frida Kahlo, one of the best artists of the twentieth century.

COCO CHANEL

ISBN: 978-1-84780-784-7

Discover the life of Coco Chanel, the famous fashion designer.

MAYA ANGELOU

ISBN: 978-1-84780-889-9

Read about Maya Angelou—one of the world's most loved writers.

AMELIA EARHART

ISBN: 978-1-84780-888-2

Learn about Amelia Earhart—the first female to fly solo over the Atlantic.

AGATHA CHRISTIE

ISBN: 978-1-78603-220-1

Meet the queen of the imaginative mystery—Agatha Christie.

MARIE CURIE

ISBN: 978-1-84780-962-9

Be introduced to Marie Curie, the Nobel Prize–winning scientist.

ROSA PARKS

ISBN: 978-1-78603-018-4

Discover the life of Rosa Parks, the first lady of the civil rights movement.

AUDREY HEPBURN
ISBN: 978-1-78603-053-5

Learn about the iconic actress and humanitarian—Audrey Hepburn.

EMMELINE PANKHURST

ISBN: 978-1-78603-019-1

Meet Emmeline Pankhurst, the suffragette who helped women get the vote.

ELLA FITZGERALD

ISBN: 978-1-78603-087-0

Meet Ella Fitzgerald, the pioneering jazz singer and musician.

ADA LOVELACE

ISBN: 978-1-78603-076-4

Read all about Ada Lovelace, the first computer programmer.

GEORGIA O'KEEFFE

ISBN: 978-1-78603-122-8

Discover the life of Georgia O'Keeffe, the famous American painter.

JANE AUSTEN

ISBN: 978-1-78603-120-4

Learn about Jane Austen, the beloved English writer.

AN OVERVIEW OF ETHIOPIA

Ethiopia is the oldest independent country in Africa and home to over a hundred different language groups. The many different ethnicities, languages, and religions of Ethiopia contribute to its exciting, melting-pot culture. About 85 percent of Ethiopians live in rural areas, practicing a simple farming lifestyle that has been the backbone of the economy for thousands of years.

By the early 1900s, Ethiopia had emerged as the leading political power in Africa. After the Ethiopian monarchy fell in 1974, however, the nation slipped into a long decline, paralyzed by civil war, famine, and a brutal military regime. Today, with a new democratic government in place, Ethiopia is heading toward a peaceful and successful future.

Opposite: **Addis Ababa, the national capital, is the largest city in Ethiopia.**

Below: **A group of Ethiopian schoolboys hangs out in the main square of Aksum.**

THE FLAG OF ETHIOPIA

The national flag of Ethiopia has three horizontal stripes of green, yellow, and red, with a circular emblem of a shining star on a blue background. The blue circle signifies peace, while the star represents the unity and future of Ethiopia's many nationalities. The green-yellow-red tricolor has been an Ethiopian national symbol since 1894. Green represents fertility; yellow symbolizes hope, justice, and equality; and red stands for sacrifice and heroism. Today, these three "Pan-African colors" also appear on the flags of African nations such as Cameroon, Ghana, Guinea, Mali, Rwanda, Senegal, and Zimbabwe.

Geography

Ethiopia lies on the Horn of Africa, an eastern part of the African continent that juts out into the Indian Ocean. A landlocked country, Ethiopia is bordered by Eritrea and Djibouti to the north, Kenya to the south, Somalia to the east, and Sudan to the west. Eritrea, which seceded from Ethiopia in 1993, and Djibouti offer the nearest seaports, along the Red Sea and the Gulf of Aden, respectively. Ethiopia has an area of 437,794 square miles (1,134,181 square kilometers), which is about the size of Texas and California combined.

The Roof of Africa

Ethiopia is known as the "Roof of Africa" because of a large plateau that stretches across the country. The Ethiopian highlands are a spectacular sight, with rocky cliffs, rolling green hills, and winding river gorges. The plateau is divided into the Western and Eastern highlands. The Western Highlands include Mount Ras Dashen, the highest peak in Ethiopia, which reaches a height of 15,158 feet (4,620 meters). In the Eastern Highlands, Mount Batu of the Bale Mountains stands at 14,127 feet (4,306 m).

Below: **The Ethiopian highlands contain both rugged hills and fertile plains.**

Above: **Salt lakes cover various parts of the Denakil Plain in northern Ethiopia.**

The Western and Eastern highlands are separated by the Great Rift Valley, a wide corridor that cuts through the Ethiopian highlands from the Kenyan border in the south to the Eritrean border in the north. The northern end of the valley funnels out into the barren Denakil Plain, while the southern end is one of the most fertile and populated areas of the country. The lowest point in Ethiopia is a depression in the Denakil Plain called the Kobar Sink, which drops to 381 feet (116 m) below sea level. Two other important regions of the Ethiopian landscape are the arid Western Lowlands, which lie west of the Western Highlands along the Sudanese border, and the Eastern Lowlands, which lie east of the Eastern Highlands and contain the desert areas of the Ogaden and the Hawd.

Rivers and Lakes

Ethiopia is the source of several rivers that carry water and silt to the countries of North and East Africa. The Genale and Wabe Shebele rivers, which originate in southwest Ethiopia, flow into Somalia, while the Blue Nile, Tekeze, and Baro rivers of western Ethiopia flow into the Nile River system in Egypt and Sudan. Water draining into the Great Rift Valley gives rise to Ethiopia's third major river system, made up of the Awash and Omo rivers. Lake Tana, the source of the Blue Nile, is the largest lake in Ethiopia.

JAMES BRUCE AND THE BLUE NILE

In 1768, British explorer James Bruce set out on a journey to discover the source of the Nile River. His travels eventually took him to Lake Tana in Ethiopia, where the Blue Nile River begins its course.

(A Closer Look, page 50)

Climate and Seasons

Ethiopia's climate varies greatly with elevation. Most Ethiopians live in the highlands or the southwestern Great Rift Valley, where the weather is cool and the average temperature is 61° Fahrenheit (16° Celsius). Temperatures in the lowlands average 82° F (28° C).

Ethiopia has three seasons. *Bega* (beh-GAH), the long dry season, lasts from September through February and is followed by *belg* (BELG), a short rainy season lasting from March through April. After a dry month of May, *kiremt* (ki-REMT), the long rainy season, begins in June and lasts through August.

Vegetation and Wildlife

The Ethiopian highlands are the wettest region in the country, and the land is covered with dense, lush forests and rich undergrowth. Drier areas, such as the lowlands and the Great Rift Valley, contain tropical forests mixed with open, grassy plains called savannas. The driest and hottest regions — the Denakil Plain, the Ogaden, and the Hawd — are generally treeless, flat stretches of grassland, rocky plains, or desert.

Above: The Omo River valley receives plenty of rainfall, making it one of the more fertile regions of Ethiopia.

WET AND DRY

The seasonal rainfall in Ethiopia varies with the altitude. Parts of the Western Highlands receive year-round rainfall totaling 80 inches (203 centimeters), while the Eastern Lowlands average about 30 inches (76 cm) of annual rainfall. The driest region of Ethiopia is the Denakil Plain, which receives less than 20 inches (51 cm) of rainfall annually.

The rough terrain of the highlands has isolated much of Ethiopian wildlife from other parts of Africa. Several of these animals, such as the walia ibex (a type of mountain goat) and the Simien fox, are endemic, or native, to Ethiopia and are found nowhere else on earth. Both the walia ibex and the Simien fox are endangered species. The lowlands of Ethiopia are home to mammals such as wild pigs, wild dogs, foxes, antelopes, hyenas, and monkeys. The animals most often associated with African safaris — lions, elephants, giraffes, and wild buffalo — are actually quite rare in Ethiopia.

Protecting Nature

Ethiopia, like its East African neighbors Kenya and Tanzania, has a reputation for breathtaking national parks and game reserves. Major national parks in Ethiopia include Bale Mountains National Park in the Eastern Highlands and Yangudi Rassa National Park along the Awash River in the Great Rift Valley. In the Western Lowlands are Gambela National Park and Omo National Park, along the Baro and Omo Rivers, respectively. Nature reserves make up almost 5 percent of the total area of Ethiopia.

BALE MOUNTAINS NATIONAL PARK

Some of Ethiopia's most unique animal species make their home in Bale Mountains National Park in the Eastern Highlands.
(A Closer Look, page 48)

Left: **A herd of cattle drinks at a watering hole in the northern Great Rift Valley.**

History

Ethiopia is over 2,000 years old, making it one of the oldest countries in the world. The first settlers of Ethiopia, in fact, may have been among the first human beings to roam the earth. Anthropologists working in Ethiopia have discovered the remains of some of the earliest human ancestors, who walked the Great Rift Valley over 4 million years ago. By 5000 B.C., the ancestors of Ethiopians were growing crops and herding animals in the Horn of Africa. In the seventh century B.C., Ethiopian settlers began trading with South Arabian merchants across the Red Sea.

Left: **The obelisks, or stone pillars, of Aksum (the former capital of Ethiopia) were built over a thousand years ago during the Aksumite empire. The Aksumites had a unique culture that fused together Arabian and African influences in their art, language, and religion.**

The Aksumite Empire

Ethiopia became a major power during the second century A.D. under the kingdom of Aksum. The Aksumites built an extensive trading empire along the Red Sea, bridging the gap between the Nile River valley and the Arabian Peninsula. Between A.D. 200 and A.D. 500, the Aksumite kingdom controlled almost the entire Horn of Africa as well as the coastal territories of what is now Yemen.

Aksum went into decline after the Persians invaded East Africa in 572. In the 1100s, the Agews, a Christian people from northern Ethiopia, established the Zagwe dynasty, which flourished under Emperor Lalibela before being toppled by a rebellion in 1270.

Left: **A famous story that may have originated during the reign of Aksum is the legend of the Queen of Sheba, also known as Makeda. In Ethiopian literature, Sheba traveled to Jerusalem and later married Solomon, the king of the Israelites. Their son, Menelik I, became the first king of Ethiopia.**

KING SOLOMON AND THE QUEEN OF SHEBA

The legend of King Solomon and the Queen of Sheba has loomed over Ethiopian politics and culture for centuries.

(A Closer Look, page 68)

The Rise of the Solomonid Dynasty

In the late thirteenth century, the Amhara people, from the kingdom of Shewa in central Ethiopia, founded the Solomonid dynasty. Claiming descent from Menelik I (the son of King Solomon of ancient Israel), the Amhara rulers pledged to unify Ethiopia under Christianity and quickly built a vast empire. Internal conflicts remained, however, because the Solomonid emperors persecuted their Muslim and Jewish subjects. In 1531, Ahmad Gran, a Muslim leader from the state of Adal (now Somalia and the Ogaden), launched a massive invasion of central Ethiopia. The Amhara managed to defeat Ahmad Gran in 1543, but only with the help of Portuguese soldiers and guns.

THE AGE OF PRINCES

By the 1700s, Ethiopia had broken up into many small kingdoms that were fought over by countless Amhara, Oromo, and Tigrayan princes and generals. The turmoil of the "Age of Princes" lasted 160 years.

The Battle of Adwa

In 1876, Emperor Yohannes IV reunited Ethiopia, but he soon faced a new enemy — the Italians, who occupied most of Eritrea by 1886. After Yohannes was killed in battle in 1889, Menelik II, the king of Shewa, became emperor of Ethiopia and negotiated the Treaty of Wichale, by which Ethiopia peacefully transferred control of Eritrea to Italy. The Italians later claimed that the treaty entitled them to intervene in both Eritrean and Ethiopian affairs, but Menelik refused to back down, and both sides prepared for war. On March 1, 1896, the Ethiopian army, numbering 100,000 men, easily defeated the Italians at the Battle of Adwa. The victory marked an important moment in African history, since Ethiopia became the only African country to have successfully defended itself against a European invasion and retained its independence.

Following the Battle of Adwa, Menelik II began reforms to modernize Ethiopia's government and infrastructure. He opened new schools and hospitals, built railroads and telephone lines, and beautified the new capital city, Addis Ababa. Ethiopia became recognized internationally.

HAILE SELASSIE

Haile Selassie was the last monarch of the Solomonid dynasty. One of Ethiopia's most powerful emperors, he reigned from 1930 to 1974.

(A Closer Look, page 62)

Below: **In this painting, Emperor Menelik II leads the Ethiopian army into battle.**

Occupation and Civil War

In 1930, Ras Tafari Makonnen declared himself emperor of Ethiopia and took the name Haile Selassie. The Italians made another attempt to take over Ethiopia in 1935, this time under the leadership of Benito Mussolini. In the resulting Italo-Ethiopian War, the Ethiopian armies were destroyed as Italy conquered Ethiopia, Eritrea, and Somaliland. Haile Selassie went into exile in 1936 and quickly appealed to the League of Nations and Great Britain for support. The Italian occupation of Ethiopia lasted until 1941, when a combined British and Ethiopian army ousted the Italian forces.

In 1952, Ethiopia and Eritrea united in an alliance that gave Eritrea its own constitution and government. The union failed, however, as the Ethiopian government dominated Eritrea for a decade before finally annexing it as a province in 1962. Civil war broke out, and opposition to Haile Selassie began to snowball. In 1971, a major drought hit Ethiopia, leaving millions of people starving, but the government ignored the famine as it fought to silence the rebellions in Eritrea. In 1974, a military committee called the Derg overthrew Haile Selassie.

Above: After five years in exile, Emperor Haile Selassie returned to Ethiopia on January 23, 1941, to help lead the fight against the Italian occupation.

Below: Italian dictator Benito Mussolini ordered the invasion of Ethiopia in 1935.

The Red Terror

The Derg declared Ethiopia a socialist state in 1974, and, by 1977, Mengistu Haile Mariam had emerged as the uncontested ruler of Ethiopia. During the "Red Terror" campaign of the late 1970s, opponents of the Derg were arrested and then executed. Soviet military aid allowed Mengistu to remain in power, despite escalating conflicts with Eritrean secessionists and the Somalis, who had invaded the Ogaden in 1977. Ethiopians continued to face hard times in the early 1980s, when severe droughts resulted in widespread famine.

New Beginnings

In 1989, rebel armies of the Eritrean People's Liberation Front (EPLF) and the Tigray People's Liberation Front (TPLF) forced Mengistu's troops out of Eritrea and Tigray. The TPLF later evolved into a larger movement called the Ethiopian People's Revolutionary Democratic Front (EPRDF). In May 1991, with his government on the verge of collapse, Mengistu fled the country, and the EPRDF took power. Eritrea declared its independence in 1993, and Ethiopia adopted a new constitution in 1994.

Above: **The TPLF was a resistance group that opposed the Mengistu regime and fought for Tigrayan autonomy in Ethiopia.**

THE ERITREAN CONFLICT

The civil war between Eritrea and Ethiopia lasted almost thirty years before Eritreans achieved independence in 1993. In 1998, however, new hostilities erupted. A cease-fire in June 2000 was followed by a peace treaty in December.

(A Closer Look, page 56)

Menelik II (1844–1913)

Menelik II was one of Ethiopia's greatest military and political leaders. He was born Sahle Mariam, a member of the royal family that ruled Shewa, a kingdom in the central Ethiopian highlands. In 1865, at the age of twenty-one, Sahle Mariam became the king of Shewa and set his eyes on the emperor's throne. In 1889, he was crowned emperor of Ethiopia and took the name Menelik II (after Menelik I, the son of King Solomon and the Queen of Sheba). Menelik II established a unified, modern state in Ethiopia by strengthening the central government, promoting trade, encouraging education, and forging strong international relations. His most historic achievement was leading the successful defense of Ethiopia against Italian invaders at the Battle of Adwa in 1896.

Menelik II

Mengistu Haile Mariam (1937–)

Mengistu Haile Mariam was the head of state of Ethiopia from 1977 to 1991, first as chairman of the Derg and then as the elected president. After serving in the Ethiopian army, Mengistu helped plot a successful military revolt against Emperor Haile Selassie in 1974. By having many of his rivals assassinated, Mengistu rose to the top of a bloody military regime. In 1987, he installed a new government and became president, but his power was fading. After facing devastating famines and a losing battle against Eritrean secessionists, Mengistu abandoned Ethiopia in 1991 and fled to Zimbabwe.

Mengistu Haile Mariam

Meles Zenawi (1955–)

Meles Zenawi is the current prime minister of Ethiopia. Raised in a middle-class, Tigrayan family, Meles studied medicine at Addis Ababa University before joining the armed struggle against the Mengistu regime. He eventually became the leader of the Tigray People's Liberation Front and then chairman of the Ethiopian People's Revolutionary Democratic Front, which drove Mengistu from power in 1991. Meles has since played a key role in drafting a new national constitution, reforming the economy, and establishing a democratic Ethiopia. He was elected chairman of the Organization of African Unity in 1995.

Meles Zenawi

Government and the Economy

After passing a new constitution in December 1994, Ethiopia became a federation of nine autonomous states and the federal capital of Addis Ababa. The nine ethnically based states are Afar; Amhara; Benshangul/Gumuz; Gambela; Harari; Oromia; Somalia; Tigray; and Southern Nations, Nationalities, and Peoples. Each state has its own president and assembly and is allowed to secede from the federation, which is officially known as the Federal Democratic Republic of Ethiopia (FDRE).

The central government of Ethiopia consists of the Federal Parliamentary Assembly and the Council of Ministers, of which the prime minister is a member. The Federal Parliamentary Assembly has two chambers — the Council of the Federation, or upper chamber, made up of 108 members elected by the state assemblies, and the Council of People's Representatives, or lower chamber, made up of 548 members elected directly by the people. Executive power of the government rests with the prime minister, who appoints the other ministers of the government and

Below: **City Hall in Addis Ababa is the office of the capital's city council.**

Above: **Tigrayans take part in a political march in Aksum.**

commands the armed forces. In 1995, the EPRDF won the national elections, and Meles Zenawi became prime minister. Girma Wolde Giorgis became president in October 2001. The president of Ethiopia has a mainly ceremonial role as the head of state.

Political Parties

The dominant political party in Ethiopia is the EPRDF. Established in 1990, the EPRDF began as an alliance of rebel groups seeking autonomy for Ethiopian ethnic groups. After the Mengistu regime collapsed, the EPRDF played a central role in shaping the new government. The main opposition party in Ethiopia is the Coalition of Alternative Forces for Peace and Democracy in Ethiopia (CAFPDE), which favors the creation of a strong central government and the preservation of Ethiopian unity. Other parties include the All-Amhara People's Organization and the Oromo Liberation Front (OLF).

THE OPPOSITION BOYCOTTS

The All-Amhara People's Organization, the CAFPDE, and the OLF all boycotted the 1995 national elections. Many opposition candidates claimed that they had been harassed by the government. Without the participation of any major opposition parties, the Ethiopian government faces a difficult challenge if it wishes to maintain its democratic goals.

An Improving Economy

The Ethiopian economy collapsed after the socialist Derg regime nationalized all farms and industries in 1975. The mismanagement of farmland resulted in food shortages, which were aggravated by civil war. By the 1980s, Ethiopia had become one of the poorest countries in the world. Since 1991, the Ethiopian government has carried out various economic reforms to repair the damage. Over 90 percent of the farms in Ethiopia are now privately run, and the government is steadily privatizing state-owned businesses. Ethiopian farmers, however, still cannot produce enough food to feed the whole nation. In 1995, Ethiopia had a food deficit of 1 million tons of grain. Generous food donations from foreign governments help to lessen the effects of Ethiopia's food shortages.

The Importance of Agriculture

Ethiopia's most valuable natural resource is its land. The highlands of Ethiopia have rich, volcanic soils that are ideal for agriculture and cattle breeding. Unfortunately, soil erosion, caused by overgrazing, deforestation, and primitive cultivation methods, has ruined many fertile areas of the Ethiopian highlands. Droughts

Above: **A farmer of the Omo River valley plows his field. More than 80 percent of the Ethiopian labor force works in agriculture.**

FAMINES

Ethiopia has suffered some of the worst famines in recent history, caused by drought, civil war, and poor land management.
(A Closer Look, page 60)

are another serious problem for Ethiopian farmers. Despite these setbacks, the government hopes to make better use of the country's arable land, only half of which is now being used by farmers.

Cash crops make up 90 percent of Ethiopia's exports. Coffee is the main cash crop, but Ethiopian farmers also grow oil seeds, wheat, barley, teff (a North African grain), cotton, tobacco, and sugarcane. Ethiopia has the largest cattle industry in Africa.

Future Potential

Ethiopia has mining reserves of gold, platinum, copper, rock salt, and marble. These resources make up only 1 percent of the nation's gross domestic product, but they are a growing sector of the economy. With its many rivers, Ethiopia also has abundant hydroelectric energy resources. Power generation stations currently lie along the Awash, Blue Nile, and Wabe Shebele rivers. Tourism is another promising industry in Ethiopia. National parks, diverse cultures, and famous historical sites (such as Aksum, Lalibela, and Gonder) make Ethiopia one of the most attractive tourist destinations in Africa.

Below: Ethiopians shop at a shoe store in Addis Ababa. Textiles and leather products are two of Ethiopia's largest industries.

People and Lifestyle

Ethiopia is a multicultural nation, with a variety of ethnic groups speaking over a hundred different African, Middle Eastern, and Mediterranean languages. Centuries of assimilation and intermarriage have blurred the distinctions among the many ethnic groups, making language and religion the most important factors in identifying the cultures of Ethiopia. The major Ethiopian language groups are the Amhara, the Tigrayans, and the Oromo. Together, they represent over two-thirds of the national population.

Language Groups

The Amhara have had a major influence on Ethiopian politics and culture over the last seven centuries. Today, the Amhara make up 24 percent of Ethiopia's population, and their language, Amharic, is the official language of the federal government. Most of the Amhara are members of the Ethiopian Orthodox Church. The state of Amhara lies in the highlands north of Addis Ababa.

Left: **An Amhara farmer enjoys the mountain air of the Ethiopian highlands.**

PEOPLES OF THE SOUTHWEST

Bordering Kenya and Sudan, the Southern Nations, Nationalities, and Peoples Regional State of Ethiopia is one of the most culturally diverse of all the federation states.

(A Closer Look, page 70)

Left: **The Oromo are the largest language group in Ethiopia.**

THE AFAR

The Denakil Plain in northern Ethiopia is a wasteland of salt flats, volcanic rock, and unbearable weather conditions — and yet the Afar people have lived there for centuries as shepherds and farmers.
(A Closer Look, page 46)

The Tigrayans of northern Ethiopia live mainly as farmers and speak two related languages, Tigrinya and Tigre. Descendants of the Aksumites, who ruled Ethiopia before the Amhara, Tigrayans make up about 8 percent of Ethiopia's population and are also adherents of the Ethiopian Orthodox Church.

The Oromo, or Galla, represent about 40 percent of the Ethiopian population. Originating from northern Kenya, the Oromo were traditionally nomadic warriors who believed in animism. After migrating to Ethiopia in the 1500s, the Oromo adopted many of the Muslim, Christian, and agricultural traditions of their neighbors. Today, the Oromo are one of the most influential and diverse peoples of Ethiopia.

A number of important minority groups are concentrated in the regions lying outside the Ethiopian highlands. Muslim groups include the Somali (of the Ogaden and the Hawd) and the Afar (of the Denakil Plain). In the southwest, the Sidamo, the Gurage, and the Konso are just three of the many peoples living in the Omo River valley. The Nilotes (named after the Nile River) are cattle herders who live on the savannas along the southeastern Sudanese border.

Below: **A young Tigrayan woman wears a decorative silver cross around her neck. Most Tigrayans are members of the Ethiopian Orthodox Church.**

Country and City

Ethiopians are mostly a rural-dwelling people. In the lowlands, Ethiopians live as nomads, traveling with herds of cattle, sheep, goats, or camels. Always on the move in search of water and pastureland, nomadic shepherds build temporary houses from animal skins and river grass. In the highlands, Ethiopians live a more settled life, either as subsistence farmers (who grow only enough food for their families to eat) or cash-crop farmers (who grow crops for profit). Highland farmers usually live in simple houses with walls made of mud and roofs made of grass or tin. In the country, most Ethiopians use wood and charcoal for their heating and cooking needs.

Rural Ethiopians looking for a new way of life often flock to Addis Ababa, the nation's capital and largest city. The political, cultural, and trading center of Ethiopia, Addis Ababa has a population of about 2.8 million people. The next largest Ethiopian city is Dire Dawa, which has about 170,000 residents. Most Ethiopian city-dwellers make their livings as small-business owners, factory workers, or merchants.

Above: **Ethiopians walk by the Lion of Judah statue in Addis Ababa.**

Family Life

Ethiopians tend to have large families. The average Ethiopian mother gives birth to five children. Due to a shortage of doctors and hospitals, however, almost 13 percent of Ethiopian children die during infancy. The average life expectancy in Ethiopia is only forty-one years.

Rural family life in Ethiopia is very male-dominated. Men do all the heavy labor — planting, weeding, and harvesting the crops, and also herding the livestock. Women help with some of the farming, but their main jobs are to cook for the family, maintain the house, and raise the children, who also must do work around the house and in the fields. As early as age five, children feed the farm animals and gather kindling for the cooking fire. Older boys help with the harvest, while older girls help cook and care for their younger siblings.

In the cities, the traditional Ethiopian family roles are changing. Women often work outside the home, and children have more opportunities for education. Even rural Ethiopian women found themselves with more responsibilities during the 1970s and 1980s, as men left home to fight in the civil war.

Below: **Family ties are strongest in rural Ethiopian communities. This family lives near Gonder, in northern Ethiopia.**

Education

With almost half the national population under the age of fifteen, education is an extremely important issue facing the Ethiopian government. Although education is free from primary school to college, the majority of Ethiopian children live in the country and do not have access to schools. Instead, they are taught by their parents at home or by religious instructors at churches, mosques, or monasteries.

Emperors Menelik II and Haile Selassie introduced Ethiopia to modern educational facilities, such as schools, universities, libraries, archives, and museums. Today, Addis Ababa University, the National School of Music, the National Library and Archives, and various arts and technical colleges are all located in the capital. Outside Addis Ababa, however, educational reform has proceeded at a much slower rate. In rural areas, schools and teachers are limited, and the enrollment of children in schools remains low. Overall, only 40 percent of Ethiopian children attend primary school, and less than 40 percent of these students move on to secondary school. Only 36 percent of Ethiopia's adult population is able to read and write.

Left: **An Ethiopian teacher encourages a young student at a primary school in Harar. English is taught in many Ethiopian schools.**

Above: **Students in a night-school class take notes during a lecture.**

For most urban Ethiopian children, primary school begins at age seven and lasts for six years. Secondary education lasts for another six years. Addis Ababa University is the country's main institution of higher learning, offering programs in business, engineering, agriculture, medicine, and law. Other important tertiary schools in Ethiopia include the Ethiopian Medical College in Gonder, the Ethiopian Agricultural College near Harar, and Mekele University.

Rural education is closely tied to either Christian or Islamic traditions. Religious schooling ranges from primary level classes to studies for the priesthood at a monastery.

Traditional culture has occasionally interfered with modern educational reform in Ethiopia. Ethiopian parents who are content with a male-dominated household are reluctant to send their daughters to school. Parents may also need their children to stay at home and work in order for the family to survive. Nevertheless, the Ethiopian government hopes to eventually build enough schools to be able to make primary and secondary education compulsory for all citizens.

Religion

Religion has strongly influenced Ethiopian family life, education, and morality. Since ancient times, Ethiopians have practiced four major religions: Christianity, Islam, animism, and Judaism.

Ethiopian Christians trace their roots back to two Syrian Christians, Frumentius and Aedesius, who arrived in Ethiopia in the fourth century A.D. Frumentius became an advisor to Ezanas, the king of the Aksumite empire, who later converted to Christianity and ordained Frumentius as the first bishop of Aksum. For over seven hundred years, until 1974, the Ethiopian Orthodox Church was the official church of Ethiopia, and it remains the most popular faith among the Amhara and the Tigrayans. Today, about 34 percent of Ethiopia's population is Ethiopian Orthodox. Other Christian groups, such as Catholics and Protestants, account for 8 percent of the population.

Left: **A young boy shades an Ethiopian Orthodox priest during a Christian festival.**

Islam first reached Ethiopia in the seventh century, as Muslim Arab traders and clerics made their way across the Red Sea. In the sixteenth century, Ethiopia's Christian monarchy narrowly escaped conquest by Muslim warrior Ahmad Gran, as Islam gained a strong foothold in the Ethiopian lowlands. Today, about 40 percent of Ethiopia's population is Muslim, including the Somali, the Afar, and the Harari. Many of the Oromo, the Sidamo, and the Gurage have also converted to Islam. The city of Harar has been a center for Muslim culture for over a thousand years.

Animism is the belief that natural objects have spirits and that these spirits influence daily life. About 12 percent of Ethiopians practice traditional, pagan religions based on animism. Many Oromo, Sidamo, and Konso believe in a sky god, who is all-powerful and the source of all life.

Numbering only a few thousand today, the Falasha, or Ethiopian Jews, are possibly the oldest religious culture in Ethiopia. Also known as Beta Israel (House of Israel), the Falasha practice a unique form of Judaism and claim to be descendants of Menelik I, the son of King Solomon and the Queen of Sheba.

Above: **Ethiopian farmers pass by a village mosque.**

HARAR

Harar is a holy Islamic city and an important hub for Ethiopian trade.
(A Closer Look, page 64)

THE FALASHA

The Falasha are one of the few Jewish peoples of Africa. Over the last thirty years, most of the Falasha have resettled in Israel, but a few settlements still survive in Ethiopia today.
(A Closer Look, page 58)

Language and Literature

Ethiopia is a land where over a hundred language groups live and work together. The major languages used in Ethiopia are Amharic, Orominga, and Tigrinya. Before 1994, the official languages of Ethiopia were Amharic and English, but this policy has changed since the new government established greater rights for minority groups. One of the responsibilities of each state government within Ethiopia is to determine an official state language. So far, the states of the Tigray, the Afar, the Somali, and the Oromo peoples have adopted new official languages for their governments. Amharic remains the official language of the

Below: **This sign is written in Amharic and English, the former official languages of Ethiopia. Today, Amharic is the working language of the federal government, while English is commonly taught in schools.**

federal government. Geez, the ancient language of the Aksumites, is commonly used in the Ethiopian Orthodox Church.

With all this language diversity, the ability to speak several languages is often a necessity in Ethiopia. Many Ethiopians can communicate in Amharic and either English or Italian in addition to their mother tongue. English is currently used as the language of instruction in high schools, and officials are planning on introducing it as a second language at the primary school level.

Amharic and Geez

Long associated with the Ethiopian monarchy, Amharic was formerly known as Lesane Negest, which means "Language of Kings." The Amharic alphabet has thirty-three characters, each of which has seven different possible pronunciations. Amharic, Tigre, Tigrinya, Geez, and South Arabian dialects belong to the same group of Semitic languages.

Geez, or Ethiopic, is the classical language of Ethiopia. The oldest Geez writings date back to the third century, during the Aksumite empire. Amharic displaced Geez as a popular language in the twelfth century, after which Geez was used only by scholars and the clergy. The most famous work of Ethiopian literature is the *Kibre Negest* (Glory of Kings), a Geez text that was written in the fourteenth century. The *Kibre Negest* chronicles the Solomonid dynasty and elaborates on the legend of the Queen of Sheba.

Left: An Ethiopian Orthodox priest holds up a cruciform-shaped Bible written in Geez.

Arts

In Ethiopia, art and religion go hand in hand. Ethiopian churches and monasteries are architectural masterpieces, often adorned with murals or stained glass windows. Religious art also comes in the form of crafts, such as the elaborate wooden or metal crosses used in Christian services and festivals. The Muslim craftsmen of Harar are famous for their silverwork and basket weaving.

Churches

Ethiopian churches are well-known for their engineering and artistic detail. The St. Mary of Zion Church, built in Aksum in 1965, features stained glass windows constructed by modern artist Afewerke Tekle. In the town of Lalibela, eleven churches stand below ground, carved out of solid rock over seven hundred years ago. The interior walls of Ethiopian churches are usually decorated with brightly colored figures painted in a distinctly Ethiopian style that is characterized by large, expressive eyes and simple, pure colors.

THE CHURCHES OF LALIBELA

Ethiopians take great pride in their beautiful churches. The churches of Lalibela are not just sacred places of worship but historical museums that preserve ancient Ethiopian cultures.
(A Closer Look, page 52)

Below: **A church painting in Addis Ababa shows a dramatic battle scene.**

Castles and Obelisks

The imposing stone castles of Gonder are another treasure of Ethiopian architecture. Built during the seventeenth and eighteenth centuries (after Emperor Fasilides had named Gonder the new capital of Ethiopia), the castles exhibit Portuguese, Aksumite, and Arabic influences in their design. The Age of Princes left most of Gonder in ruins, but the remains of numerous palaces, cathedrals, and bathhouses still stand. Ethiopian Orthodox priests hold services at the Debre Berhan Selassie Church, one of Gonder's few surviving churches.

The legacy of the Aksumite emperors is evident in the towering obelisks of Aksum, the former capital of Ethiopia. An obelisk is a four-sided, tapering pillar, usually made from a single piece of stone; it often has religious or historical inscriptions. The Egyptians built the first obelisks over four thousand years ago, and their design was later adopted by Middle Eastern and African peoples. Some 126 obelisks once stood erect in the main square of Aksum. Today, many of the monuments lie broken on the ground, including one that measures 110 feet (34 m) in length

Above: **The castles of Gonder are one of Ethiopia's major tourist sites. Gonder was the capital of the Ethiopian empire between 1632 and 1855.**

Below: **The main square of Aksum is marked by over a hundred obelisks.**

Music and Dance

Song and dance are important aspects of Ethiopian religious worship and social customs. Unordained clergy of the Ethiopian Orthodox Church, known as the *debtera* (deb-tuh-RAH), are responsible for chanting, dancing, and playing music during worship services. The melodies of these chants were composed almost 1,500 years ago by an Ethiopian musician named Yared. Ethiopian Orthodox priests have since compiled the chants into six volumes. The debtera perform these chants from memory, often improvising on the melodies.

Minstrels, or *azmari* (az-MAH-ree), have traditionally roamed the Ethiopian countryside singing folk songs at festivals or village gatherings. They are also known for their political commentaries, which they express in song. The azmari's main instrument is the lyre, which is a stringed instrument similar to a harp.

Ethiopians often celebrate weddings, childbirths, and harvests with traditional dances. The Karo of the Omo River valley and the Somali of the Ogaden use courtship dances as a way for men and women to choose their partners in marriage.

Above: **Ethiopian musicians and dancers celebrate Maskal, a Christian holiday.**

Handicrafts

Handicrafts such as jewelry, basketry, pottery, weaving, and leatherwork are well-established artistic traditions in Ethiopia. Increased tourism has turned some craft-making into small industries, but Ethiopian handicrafts are still a mainstay of street markets and village traders.

Different cultural groups in Ethiopia specialize in different arts and crafts. The Harari are expert silversmiths and basket weavers; the *mesob* (meh-SOHB), a large, colorful basket used by Ethiopians as an eating table, is a popular Harari craft. The Afar of the Denakil Plain are known for the beautiful leather sheaths that encase their long, curved daggers, while the Konso of the Omo River valley are respected weavers, potters, and blacksmiths. Falasha artists are known for their pottery.

Above: A Karo man wears fresh body paint.

Body Painting

A striking art form among the Surma and Karo peoples of southwestern Ethiopia is body painting, which is usually done in preparation for a ceremony or dance. The paint, made of chalk, iron oxide, and water, is applied to the body with one's fingertips.

Below: Three Ethiopian craftswomen weave together straw to make baskets.

Leisure and Festivals

In rural Ethiopia, leisure time is spent pursuing simple pleasures, such as spending time with the family or entertaining guests at home. A favorite Ethiopian social activity is chatting with friends over home-brewed coffee. For nomadic peoples, such as the Afar and the Somali, privacy and free time are scarce. Since nomadic families usually travel in clans, any leisure time available for games or celebrations is shared by the entire community.

Ethiopian cities offer more outlets for leisure, such as parks, restaurants, movie theaters, and shopping centers. Addis Ababa has many affordable pleasures, such as the Mercato (one of the largest open-air markets in Africa), a zoo, museums, and sports arenas. The capital is also just a short drive from the lakes of the Great Rift Valley, where Ethiopians enjoy water sports, hiking, and bird-watching.

Games

Ethiopians have their own traditional games that are similar to Western games such as checkers, jacks, and hide-and-seek. A popular African game is mancala, which Ethiopians call *gebeta*

Below: **Urban Ethiopians enjoy going to the movies to spend their leisure time.**

Above: **Two Ethiopian competitors square off in a game of mancala, one of the most popular games played in Africa.**

(geh-beh-TAH). Mancala is a two-player game that originated in Egypt. The board is usually divided into twelve bins split into two rows, or six bins per player. (Other versions of the game have ten bins split into two rows of five.) Each bin contains four stones. Each player also has a mancala, or storage bin, on the right of his six smaller bins that is empty at the start of the game. Through a series of maneuvers, players move stones from bin to bin, including their own and their opponent's mancalas, in their play. The winner is the player who collects the most stones in his or her mancala.

Oral Tradition

Many rural Ethiopian peoples still practice an oral tradition in which storytelling and poetry recitals are forms of entertainment. The Somali of the Ogaden did not have a written language until 1973. Instead of books, the Somali relied on word of mouth for works of literature to be passed on to the next generations.

Sports

Italian colonists introduced Eritrea to soccer in the early 1900s, and Ethiopians quickly picked up the sport from their northern neighbors. The Ethiopian Football Federation was founded in 1943, and Ethiopia formed the African Football Confederation with Egypt and Sudan in 1956. Today, soccer is the most popular sport in Ethiopia. In the city streets and the open countryside, young Ethiopians love to play pickup soccer games. Professional soccer matches in Addis Ababa attract huge crowds of spectators.

Other popular sports in Ethiopia are running, volleyball, basketball, tennis, swimming, and cycling. Traditional Ethiopian

Below: **An Ethiopian soccer match gets underway in the city of Dire Dawa.**

sports include *ganna* (gehn-NAH), which is similar to field hockey, and *guks* (GOOGS), which is a joust between armed men on horseback.

Going the Distance

Ethiopia has produced some of the fastest long-distance runners in the world. Abebe Bikila inspired a long line of Ethiopian champion runners. At the 1968 Olympic Games, Mamo Wolde won the gold medal in the marathon and the silver medal in the 10,000-meter run. At the 1972 Olympic Games, Mamo won the bronze medal in the marathon. Miruts Yifter won the bronze

ABEBE BIKILA

Marathon runner Abebe Bikila was one of Ethiopia's greatest athletes. He won the gold medal in the marathon event at the 1960 and 1964 Olympic Games.
(A Closer Look, page 44)

medal in the 10,000-meter run. In 1980, Miruts won Olympic gold medals in the 5,000- and 10,000-meter races.

At the 1992 Olympic Games, a young Ethiopian woman named Derartu Tulu won the 10,000-meter race and became the first African woman to win an Olympic gold medal. In 1996, Ethiopian runner Fatuma Roba became the first African woman to capture the Olympic gold medal in the marathon.

Haile Gebrselassie won the 10,000-meter run in 1996, setting an Olympic record. He won the event again in 2000. Millon Wolde won the 5,000-meter run in 2000, and Gezahgne Abera won the marathon in 2000.

Left: Ethiopian long-distance runner Miruts Yifter *(right)* won two gold medals in the 1980 Olympic Games in Moscow.

Religious Holidays

Ethiopians celebrate a number of religious holidays during the year. Ethiopia's official calendar is the Julian calendar, which consists of twelve months of thirty days and a thirteenth month of five days (six days on a leap year).

Ethiopian Orthodox Christians observe more than two hundred annual fast days, during which they abstain from eating meat, eggs, and dairy products. Ganna, or Christmas, falls on January 7. The morning of Ganna is spent in worship at church, while the afternoon is reserved for a feast with family and friends. The afternoon festivities usually include a spirited game of ganna. Timkat, or Epiphany, is the most important Christian holiday in Ethiopia, falling on January 19. Timkat commemorates the day the Three Wise Men, or Magi, found the infant Jesus in Bethlehem.

Ethiopians celebrate Maskal, or the Finding of the True Cross, on September 27. Maskal is a Christian holiday that also celebrates the arrival of spring. Maskal celebrations include marching

Above: **Ethiopian Christian priests celebrate Ganna, or Christmas, in Lalibela.**

TIMKAT

Timkat, or Epiphany, is a spectacular religious event in Ethiopia. Christian priests wearing shimmering robes lead a long procession of musicians, chanters, dancers, and worshipers.
(A Closer Look, page 72)

parades with floats, dancers, and musicians. The most exciting Maskal tradition is constructing a huge bonfire around a long pole, or *demera* (dem-uh-RAH), that has been decorated with eucalyptus branches and yellow maskal daisies.

Ethiopian Muslims celebrate the end of Ramadan, the annual month of fasting, with a day-long celebration called Eid al-Fitr, the Feast of the Breaking of the Fast. Other important Muslim holidays include Eid al-Adha (Feast of the Sacrifice) and Mawlid (the anniversary of the birthday of Prophet Muhammad).

Secular Holidays

Enkutatash, the Ethiopian New Year, falls on September 11 and signals the end of kiremt, the long rainy season. Ethiopian families cover their floors with freshly cut grass and light fires in their homes to welcome the new year. A fun children's holiday is Buhe (August 19), which is similar to Halloween. Boys and girls go door to door, bearing torches and singing in return for bread or money.

Two more important national holidays are Victory of Adwa Day (March 2), which commemorates Ethiopia's victory at the Battle of Adwa in 1896, and National Day (May 28), which is the anniversary of the fall of the Mengistu regime.

Left: **An Ethiopian dressed as an ancient warrior marches in a Maskal procession. The story surrounding Maskal goes back to the early fourth century A.D., when the Roman empress Helena allegedly discovered the cross on which Christ was crucified. Legend has it that she gave a piece of the cross to the Aksumite emperor in order to thank him for protecting Christians in his kingdom.**

Food

Ethiopia has a reputation for spicy cuisine and home-style cooking. Ethiopian cooks season their food generously with red pepper, garlic, ginger, cloves, cinnamon, nutmeg, and coriander, making their dishes both fiery and delicious. Another essential ingredient of the meal is family hospitality, one of the most important values in Ethiopian culture. Even a poor Ethiopian family with hardly enough to eat will graciously offer a visitor coffee or fruit.

Breaking the Bread

The basic part of any Ethiopian meal is a thin, sour pancake called *injera* (in-JAYR-ah). Injera flour is made from teff, a grain that is native to Ethiopia. The batter is slightly fermented, which makes injera taste a bit like sourdough bread. A typical Ethiopian meal has a piece of injera laid directly on the mesob, a large basket used as a low table. The injera serves as both the bread and the plate of the meal. Ethiopians ladle a few spoonfuls of *wat* (WEHT), a spicy stew, on top of the injera. The most popular kind of wat is *doro wat* (DOHR-oh weht), which is made with chicken; other variations

HOME COOKING

A lot of behind-the-scenes work goes into a home-cooked Ethiopian meal. Women do all the domestic work in most Ethiopian homes.
(A Closer Look, page 66)

Below: A rural Ethiopian woman cooks injera over a charcoal stove.

Above: **Vendors sell fresh fruits and vegetables at a market in Addis Ababa.**

contain beef, lamb, fish, lentils, chickpeas, or beans. Diners sit closely around the mesob and use the fingers of their right hand to tear off a small piece of injera, which is then used to scoop up the wat. It is bad manners to dip one's fingers into the wat or to touch one's mouth while eating.

Most Ethiopians eat plain injera for breakfast, but foods such as baked bread, eggs, or porridge are also common. Lunch might include injera with vegetables or just a piece of sugarcane to chew on. Ethiopians eat their main meal of the day in the evening.

Drinks

Coffee is the most popular drink in Ethiopia, and Ethiopian coffee beans are prized around the world. For each pot of coffee, an Ethiopian family will roast and grind the beans in a traditional ceremony. Ethiopians take their coffee black, usually with sugar or honey. The resulting drink is rich, sweet, and wonderfully aromatic. Ethiopians also enjoy drinking *tej* (TEHJ), a wine made from honey, and *tella* (TEH-lah), a kind of beer made from barley, corn, or wheat.

COFFEE

Ethiopia is famous for its coffee, which is a major export. Coffee drinking is an age-old social pleasure among Ethiopians.
(*A Closer Look, page 54*)

A CLOSER LOOK AT ETHIOPIA

Ethiopia has made international headlines because of its civil war and famines, but the nation has also had glorious moments, such as the Olympic victories of Abebe Bikila and the recent birth of a democratic government. With tourism on the rise, foreigners are discovering Ethiopia's vast treasures, such as Bale Mountains National Park, the Blue Nile River, the churches of Lalibela, and some of the best coffee in the world.

Although Ethiopian culture is often associated with the Amhara, whose language, religion, and customs dominated the region for centuries, immigrant peoples have always been a part of Ethiopia's identity. In 1994, Ethiopia adopted a new constitution that granted autonomy to all the major peoples of Ethiopia. The world now recognizes Ethiopia as a multiethnic democracy that has united numerous African cultures, including the Oromo, the Tigrayans, the Somali, the Konso, the Hamer-Banna, and the Afar.

Opposite: **An Ethiopian family sells baskets in a Gonder market.**

Below: **Two schoolgirls look forward to their day in class.**

43

Abebe Bikila

Ethiopian marathon runner Abebe Bikila was one of the greatest athletes the world has ever known. Abebe won the marathon at the 1960 and 1964 Olympic Games and proved to the world that Ethiopians are capable of legendary achievements.

Abebe was born in 1932 in a small town outside Addis Ababa. The son of a shepherd, he eventually enlisted in the army in 1952. One day, after seeing a parade of Ethiopian athletes who had just participated in the 1956 Olympic Games, Abebe made up his mind to train for the Olympic Games. At the national athletic championship for the Ethiopian armed forces, Abebe won three running events and earned his ticket to the 1960 Olympic Games.

Below: **Abebe Bikila draws away from Abdesselem Rhadi of Morocco near the finish line of the marathon at the 1960 Olympic Games in Rome. Abebe won the gold medal.**

Making Olympic History

Abebe was unknown outside Ethiopia and considered a long shot to win the 1960 Olympic marathon in Rome. Tied for the lead throughout much of the race, he broke ahead in the last 1,000 meters

Left: **Abebe Bikila**
(front) **trains in Tokyo,**
Japan, for the 1964
Olympic Games.
He became the first
athlete to win two
Olympic gold medals
in the marathon event.

and finished first to capture the gold medal. His time set a new
world record — an amazing feat considering that he had run the
race barefoot. After winning the race, Abebe sauntered around
the track for a victory lap, proudly holding up the Ethiopian flag.

In 1964, Abebe underwent an emergency appendectomy
just one month before the Olympic Games in Tokyo, Japan. His
chances of winning a second Olympic marathon looked dismal,
but Abebe overcame the odds and became the first person to
win two Olympic gold medals in the marathon. For his second
Olympic victory, he wore running shoes.

At the 1968 Olympic Games in Mexico City, Abebe was
forced to drop out after 10 miles (16 km) because of a leg fracture.
A year later, a serious automobile accident left him a paraplegic,
thus ending his athletic career. When he died in 1973, Abebe was
given an enormous state funeral in Ethiopia.

The Afar

The Denakil Plain, at the northern end of the Great Rift Valley, is one of the hottest and driest places on earth. With daytime temperatures reaching 145° F (63° C) and no rainfall for three-quarters of the year, these lowlands present great obstacles to human habitation. Only the Afar — a tough, proud, nomadic people — have managed to survive the Denakil Plain's extreme geographic conditions.

Above: **An Afar girl shows off her brightly colored, beaded jewelry and carefully braided hair.**

Life on the Desert

Numbering over 1.1 million people, the Afar are believed to have migrated to the Denakil Plain from southern Ethiopia. Today, the Afar are spread out across Djibouti, northeastern Ethiopia, and the Eritrean coast. Afar Regional State (one of Ethiopia's nine states) has autonomy from the central government and its own official language, Saho. Assayita, on the banks of the Awash River, is the most important Afar settlement of the state. It is the capital of the Sultan of Aussa and a regional center for Islam, which most of the Afar practice.

The Afar are famous for their physical stamina, their bravery, and their hostility toward intruders, which have made them greatly feared by outsiders. Most Afar are nomadic herders who raise goats or camels and live in portable shelters made of brushwood and mats. Every year, during the intense heat of the dry season, they migrate to the Awash, the only reliable water source in the region. The Denakil Plain has only one rainy season (lasting from November through January), during which the Afar move up into the hills to avoid the flooding Awash. The Afar also work as farmers, fishermen, and salt miners. Mine workers often stay in the same place for long periods of time, living in huts made of salt blocks. Agriculture is very limited because much of the Denakil Plain consists of solid volcanic rock covered by a thick crust of salt.

Milk is the most important part of the Afar diet; meat is eaten only on special occasions. Afar nomads trade butter or livestock to obtain any goods they cannot grow or make themselves. Since the Afar region has little arable land, grain is extremely scarce, and most of the Afar nomads do not use it to make bread. Instead, they simply roast and then eat the grains whole.

Opposite: **Afar herders gather at a market in the Denakil Plain.**

Bale Mountains National Park

Ethiopia has ten national parks, thirteen wildlife sanctuaries, and eighteen game reserves, which cover a total area of 21,320 square miles (55,218 square km). Bale Mountains National Park, located south of Addis Ababa in the Bale Mountains, is one of Ethiopia's most important wildlife preservation areas. The park protects the higher reaches of the Bale Mountains, where juniper forests and alpine grasslands provide shelter for many native mammals. Ethiopia has a surprisingly high number of endemic species that are found nowhere else on earth. Of 260 mammal species found in the country, about fifty are endemic to Ethiopia.

Natives and Neighbors

A prized inhabitant of Bale Mountains National Park is the mountain nyala, a large antelope endemic to Ethiopia, with a population of about 4,000. Discovered in 1908, the nyala is now listed as an endangered species.

Below: **The Bale Mountains are a beautiful highland habitat for some of the rarest animals in the world.**

Left: **The Simien fox is a rare canine species found only in Ethiopia.**

Another endangered endemic species found in the Bale Mountains is the Simien fox, the rarest of the world's canine species. Only a few thousand Simien foxes are believed to exist, with almost 75 percent of these living in Bale Mountains National Park. Similar to a jackal, the Simien fox stands about 24 inches (60 cm) high and sports a red coat with a black tail and a white belly and throat. Its main prey are rodents and other small animals. The Simien fox was once common in the Ethiopian highlands, but its numbers have decreased dramatically in the twentieth century, probably due to diseases such as distemper and rabies.

One of the Simien fox's primary meals is the giant mole rat, a large rodent that grows up to 10 inches (25 cm) long and lives underground, surfacing only to gather its food (mainly grains and grasses). After quickly collecting a stash of plants, the giant mole rat stores it in an underground chamber, one of many within an extensive system of tunnels. The mole rat's constant burrowing leaves the ground riddled with holes, which sometimes give its location away to aboveground predators.

Other mammals found in Bale Mountains National Park include the colobus monkey, the gelada baboon, the Abyssinian lion, the spotted hyena, and Menelik's bushbuck (an antelope that lives in woody mountainous areas).

James Bruce and the Blue Nile

Over the last three centuries, Africa has attracted numerous adventurers and treasure hunters, their curiosity stirred by tales of ancient kingdoms, exotic peoples, and immense riches. For British explorer James Bruce (1730–1794), the allure of Africa was the mighty Nile River, the longest river in the world. In 1768, he set out on an expedition to find the source of the Nile. His journey through Egypt, Ethiopia, and what is now Eritrea remains one of the most famous African adventure stories of all time.

An Explorer's Tale

In 1763, Bruce was appointed British consul in Algiers (now the capital of Algeria). He spent time traveling in North Africa and Syria, but his dream was to go to Ethiopia, where he believed he could locate the source of the Blue Nile. At that time, the Blue Nile tributary was believed to be the source of the Nile River.

In 1768, starting in Cairo, Egypt, Bruce followed the Nile south to the city of Aswan. He then redirected his route along the Red Sea, continuing southward and arriving at Mitsiwa, on the Ethiopian coast (now Eritrea), in 1769. On February 14, 1770, he reached Gonder, which was then the Ethiopian capital.

Bruce's expedition was very dangerous. The Ethiopian empire had fallen apart, and the countryside had become a battlefield for political rivals. Bruce soldiered on, determined in his quest to trace the river to its source. Finally, on November 14, 1770, he discovered the headwaters of the Blue Nile at Lake Tana. Convinced that he had found the Nile's source, Bruce returned to England in 1774 and began writing his memoirs of Africa, *Travels to Discover the Source of the Nile*. His stories aroused controversy, however, because no other explorers had seen this part of Africa. Later expeditions confirmed Bruce's observations of Ethiopia.

In 1858, another British explorer, John Speke (1827–1864), discovered Lake Victoria, the source of another Nile tributary called the White Nile. Speke correctly claimed that the White Nile was the true source of the Nile. Although Bruce has been discredited as the discoverer of the Nile's source, his adventures are still celebrated by historians and travelers.

Above: Born in Scotland, James Bruce became a legendary explorer of Eastern Africa in the late eighteenth century.

Opposite: The Blue Nile River begins at a waterfall known as the Abay (or Tissisat) near Lake Tana.

The Churches of Lalibela

Ethiopia is a land of beautiful churches. Unlike Western-style churches, the typical Ethiopian church is circular or octagonal in shape and divided into three concentric sections. The center area, accessible only to priests, is a sanctum where sacred relics are kept. The middle ring, where communion takes place, is reserved for worshipers who have fully complied with restrictions ordered by the church (such as observing certain fasting days); the remaining worshipers occupy the outermost ring.

Solid as a Rock

The most famous churches in Ethiopia are the rock-hewn churches of Lalibela, which are more than seven hundred years old. Carved out of solid granite, these eleven churches are a marvel of design and workmanship.

Below: **Ethiopian Christians celebrate Timkat at the House of Giorgis, one of the eleven rock-hewn churches in Lalibela.**

A visitor to Lalibela could easily miss the churches entirely, since they are below ground. All that gives away their presence are the priests who emerge from the ground as they exit the tunnels leading down to the churches. The largest of the Lalibela churches, the House of Medhane Alem (Savior of the World), is 109 feet (33 m) long, 77 feet (23 m) wide, and 35 feet (10 m) high. The House of Giorgis (St. George) features a cruciform shape and a narrow courtyard below its towering walls. The churches are connected by a network of underground passageways.

The town of Lalibela, originally called Roha, was the traditional capital of the Zagwe dynasty, which ruled Ethiopia during the twelfth and thirteenth centuries A.D. Emperor Lalibela reigned from 1185 to 1225 and ordered the construction of the rock-hewn churches in Roha. The churches became so famous that the town was renamed Lalibela. Today, Lalibela remains Ethiopia's holiest religious site, attracting thousands of pilgrims on Christian holidays such as Ganna and Timkat. Of the town's 5,600 people, more than 1,000 are priests.

Above: **Abba Libanos is part of a group of Lalibela churches that were carved from a single rock hill.**

Coffee

Coffee is the most important cash crop in Ethiopia, accounting for over 60 percent of the country's export earnings. Most Ethiopian coffee farmers work on small plots of land in the southwestern areas of the country. In fact, some scholars claim that the word *coffee* comes from Kefa, the name of a former southern Ethiopian province, where coffee trees grow wild. Ethiopians may have invented brewed coffee, before passing it along to the cultures of Arabia, India, Indonesia, and South America. Today, coffee is the

second most popular beverage in the world (after tea) and is consumed by almost 2 billion people every day.

Above: **A young Ethiopian woman displays a tray of dried coffee beans.**

The Fruits of Labor

Coffee is a difficult crop to grow successfully. After planting the seeds, farmers must carefully tend the plants for three to five years before they reach full size. After flowering, a coffee tree begins to grow fleshy, marble-sized fruit. Each fruit, or cherry, contains two coffee seeds, or beans, covered by a silvery skin. When ripe, the cherries turn from green to bright red and are sweet to the taste.

Coffee Culture

Ethiopians appreciate coffee not just as a cash crop but as a cultural tradition. Coffee enthusiasts are everywhere in Ethiopia, and they take their coffee much more seriously than the millions of other coffee drinkers in the world, many of whom want nothing more than a morning dose of caffeine.

A traditional Ethiopian way of welcoming a guest is a coffee ceremony. The hostess of the house spreads a colorful rug or mat on the floor, over which fresh green grass and flowers are strewn. While roasting the coffee beans over an open fire or charcoal burner, the hostess invites the guests to waft some of the fragrant

smoke toward themselves to savor the aroma. The roasted beans are then crushed with a mortar and pestle and added, with boiling water, to a serving pot. As the coffee steeps, the hostess places the pot in a decorative holder and lets the grounds settle to the bottom of the pot. The youngest child in the house is then summoned to serve the guests, starting with the eldest in the room. Fresh bread is often served with the hot coffee.

The first round of the coffee ceremony is followed by two more rounds, and the entire process may last up to two hours. As the guests relax over their cups of coffee, conversation flows and friendships deepen.

Above: **Two Ethiopian women prepare a fresh pot of coffee.**

The Eritrean Conflict

The Eritrean conflict is one of the most important events of modern Ethiopian history. Spanning three decades, the civil war between Ethiopia and Eritrea severely affected the economies, governments, and peoples of these two neighboring territories. Over 100,000 people were killed and over a million refugees fled the region before the Eritrean People's Liberation Front (EPLF) finally took control of Eritrea in 1991.

Prized Territory

Merchants always considered Eritrea a strategic region because it linked the Nile River valley and Ethiopia to trade routes along the Red Sea. Since the Aksumite empire, Eritrea has been a crossroads of foreign cultures — especially the Islamic culture of Arab traders. Today, Eritreans are divided evenly between Muslims and Christians. Although Eritrea and Ethiopia share some common ethnic groups, their respective cultures are very different.

Below: **Shipping boats dock at a port in Mitsiwa, on the northern coast of Eritrea. Eritrea's access to the Red Sea has long been coveted by Ethiopian rulers.**

Above: **Soldiers of the Tigray People's Liberation Front (TPLF) joined forces with Eritrean rebels in the late 1980s.**

Federation, Fallout, and Independence

In 1952, the United Nations joined Eritrea and Ethiopia in a federation by which Eritrea retained its right to self-government. The federation was supposed to preserve Eritrean autonomy and culture, but it actually enabled Ethiopia to take advantage of its smaller, weaker neighbor. In 1962, Eritrea was stripped of its federal status and made a province of Ethiopia. During the mid-1960s, the Eritrean Liberation Front (ELF), a resistance group founded by Eritrean Muslims, waged a guerrilla war against the Ethiopian military in western Eritrea. By 1977, the ELF and the EPLF (a nationalist group that had emerged in 1974) controlled most of Eritrean territory.

The Ethiopian government turned to the Soviet Union for help. Using Soviet arms, the Ethiopian army recaptured Eritrea in 1978, but the nationalist struggle continued. The EPLF displaced the ELF and then allied itself with rebel movements in Ethiopia during the late 1980s. The civil war finally ended in 1991, when Ethiopia's Derg regime collapsed, and the EPLF liberated Eritrea. After holding a national referendum, Eritrea proclaimed its official independence in 1993

PEACE TREATY

The Eritrean conflict resurfaced in 1998, when a border dispute resulted in the Eritrean invasion of northern Ethiopia. Ethiopian forces invaded Eritrean territory in 2000. A cease-fire and a peace treaty were signed later that year.

The Falasha

The Falasha, or Beta Israel (House of Israel), are an ancient Ethiopian Jewish people who are now concentrated in Israel. The Falasha follow most Jewish traditions, but they do not recognize the Talmud, the authoritative body of Jewish law and tradition that is considered one of the foundations of Judaism. Another difference between the Falasha and other Jews of the world is that the Falasha's scriptures are written in Geez, not Hebrew.

The remaining Falasha in Ethiopia generally live in their own villages or in separate communities within Christian villages.

Above: **A teacher instructs his students at a rural Falasha school.**

Each Falasha settlement has its own synagogue, which is used for worship services, schooling, and gatherings. Most of the Falasha continue to live in traditional ways, working as blacksmiths, weavers, potters, and tanners.

A History of Isolation

Although the Falasha trace their lineage to Menelik I, scholars date the roots of the Falasha to around the first century A.D., when Jews from Arabia probably crossed the Red Sea and converted a number of Ethiopians to Judaism. In the fourth century, the

Aksumite kingdom converted to Christianity, and the Falasha were forced to settle near Lake Tana. Over the next thousand years, Christian rulers persecuted the Falasha, who chose to maintain their Jewish faith and endure the consequences, rather than convert to Christianity or flee Ethiopia. Since the Falasha remained isolated in a Christian kingdom, most of the world was not even aware of their existence until the late 1800s. By the early twentieth century, some 20,000 Falasha villagers were living in northern Ethiopia.

In 1974, the Derg regime took power in Ethiopia, and people around the world became concerned about the fate of the Ethiopian Jewish community. Civil war, famine, and a cruel military regime

Above: **This Falasha synagogue stands in a village near Lake Tana.**

Left: **Ethiopians adjust to their new surroundings at a Falasha immigrant center in Israel.**

threatened the welfare of the peaceful Falasha. In 1984 and 1991, the Israeli government carried out two evacuation programs, known as Operation Moses and Operation Solomon, which airlifted almost 30,000 Falasha from Ethiopian refugee camps into Israel. Only a few thousand Falasha remain in Ethiopia.

The Falasha have had a mixed experience in Israel. While some Israeli communities were reluctant to accept them, others were proud to welcome the Falasha to Israel. Most Falasha immigrants have found the transition to Israeli society difficult, but they are thankful for the opportunity to start a new life.

Famines

Over the last thirty years, Ethiopia has been hit hard by famines. A famine is an extreme shortage of food resulting from either natural or human events. The major causes of famine in Ethiopia have been drought, soil erosion, civil war, and poor land reforms.

In the early 1970s, a severe drought in northern Ethiopia resulted in massive crop failures. Over one million Ethiopians died from starvation and disease. The famine also caused a mass migration, as peasants abandoned their villages in search of food. A scandal erupted in 1973, when Emperor Haile Selassie denied that the famine existed so as not to disrupt tourism in Ethiopia.

Famines continued throughout the Derg regime, as the civil war with Eritrea raged on and droughts hit Ethiopia in the late 1970s and mid-1980s. In 1975, the Derg began a land reform

Left: **Ethiopian drought victims receive food at a refugee center.**

Left: An Ethiopian schoolboy plants a tree seedling. Trees help keep the soil from eroding.

PREVENTING SOIL EROSION

Although droughts are difficult to control and predict, soil erosion can be prevented by careful farming methods and forest conservation. With better land management, Ethiopia will eventually be able to grow enough food to meet the demands of its people without depleting its soil or its forests.

program in which fields were divided up equally among farmers. In order to get higher crop yields, the farmers overcultivated the land and depleted the soil, causing their harvests to decline. The famine worsened as state-owned industries failed, and the government spent increasing amounts to fight the war.

The famine of 1984 left more than 15 percent of the Ethiopian population at risk of starvation. The Derg tried to solve the problem by resettling over 600,000 people from northern Ethiopia into the less populated south and west. The government, however, could not afford the cost of food, housing, and medical care for such a large number of people. The state of emergency ended in 1985, as grain donations from abroad finally reached Ethiopian refugees.

ANOTHER FAMINE

In 1991, the Ethiopian People's Revolutionary Democratic Front (EPRDF) took power and reformed the entire government. During this period of transition, Ethiopia's economy suffered, and another famine swept the country in 1994. In 2002–2003, a combination of drought and low crop prices caused serious food shortages.

61

Haile Selassie

Haile Selassie, Ethiopia's last emperor, was born Ras (Prince) Tafari Makonnen in 1892. During the reign of Menelik II, the young Ras Tafari was appointed governor of Harar and Awasa. After the emperor's death in 1913, the crown passed to Menelik's grandson, Lij Yasu, and then to Menelik's daughter, Zauditu, in 1917. She ruled with the assistance of Ras Tafari, who was proclaimed heir apparent to the throne.

Ras Tafari was an ambitious leader who believed in forging alliances with other countries. He became the first Ethiopian ruler to travel to Europe, and he was responsible for Ethiopia's acceptance into the League of Nations in 1923. In 1928, Tafari took the title of *negus* (NEE-gus), or king. After Zauditu's death in 1930, he was crowned emperor and adopted the name Haile

Left: **Emperor Haile Selassie went to the United Kingdom for a state visit in October 1954.**

Selassie (Might of the Trinity). One of Haile Selassie's first acts as emperor was decreeing a new constitution that limited the powers of the Ethiopian parliament. Until the end of his reign in 1974, Haile Selassie essentially controlled the Ethiopian government.

In 1935, Italy invaded Ethiopia, hoping to avenge its defeat at the Battle of Adwa in 1896. Unable to compete with Italy's military, Haile Selassie fled the country and called upon the League of Nations for help. Although the league refused to intervene, Ethiopia found an ally in Great Britain once World War II began in 1939. In 1941, an army of British soldiers and Ethiopian exiles successfully invaded Ethiopia. Upon his return to Addis Ababa, Haile Selassie was renamed emperor. He had lost some of his supporters during his time in exile, but he still managed to amass great political power as he continued his mission to modernize Ethiopia. The emperor's most important achievements were major land reforms in 1942 and 1944, the emancipation of slaves in 1942, and the granting of universal suffrage in 1955. In 1963, Haile Selassie helped establish the Organization of African Unity.

The pace of economic reforms was still too slow for most rural Ethiopians, who desperately needed better land reform. Haile Selassie's corrupt government was also slow in aiding famine victims. In 1974, the military overthrew Haile Selassie, who was put under house arrest until his death in 1975

Harar

The desert city of Harar, located northwest of the Ogaden, is the center of Muslim culture in Ethiopia. The original city, founded in the seventh century, was built 100 miles (161 km) south of the present location. As the capital of Adal, a former Islamic state that rose to power in the sixteenth century, Harar became one of the most important Muslim settlements in East Africa. In 1543, however, Adal ruler Ahmad Gran (Ahmad the Left-Handed) was killed in battle against the Amhara, and the Muslim state quickly collapsed. In 1577, Harar was relocated to its present site, pushed out by the expanding Amhara and Oromo settlements.

Situated between the Somali port of Berbera and the Ethiopian highlands, Harar developed into a busy trading city during the 1600s and 1700s. The city also evolved into a distinctively Islamic state. Only Muslims (mainly the Harari and Somali) were allowed to enter the walled, inner city, while non-Muslims occupied the outer areas. In 1854, British explorer Richard Burton became the first surviving European visitor behind the walls of Harar, where he spent ten days under the watchful eye of the emir.

Below: **Harar is famous for its intimate street markets, where people can buy goods such as grain, coffee, spices, pottery, and basketry.**

Above: **Harar's colorful streets attract traders, tourists, artists, and Muslim pilgrims.**

Egyptian forces invaded Harar in 1875 and occupied it for about ten years. In 1887, Menelik II annexed Harar to the Ethiopian empire, and he appointed Ras Tafari to govern the city in 1910. Although the official religion of Ethiopia was Christianity until 1974, Harar survived as a thriving Muslim community. Today, the city of Harar is the capital of Harari Regional State, one of the nine states in the Ethiopian federation. The population of Harar is about 130,000 people.

The strong Muslim character of Harar is evidenced by the ninety-nine mosques that grace the city. Most of the city's Muslim population still lives in old Harar, which is filled with bustling markets and traditional houses with red granite walls. The Harari make a living as traders, while the Oromo, Somali, and Amhara settlers work as farmers and shepherds in the surrounding countryside. Harari artists and craftsmen are famous for their basket weaving and silversmithing. Residents of Harar speak Harari (which is related to Amharic), Amharic, Somali, Orominga, or Arabic.

Home Cooking

Preparing dinner is an all-day affair in an Ethiopian household. For women living in rural areas, cooking consumes much of their time and is an exhausting task. International relief workers have suggested that an effective way to aid economic development in Ethiopia is to provide equipment that will make it easier for women to cook and prepare food.

On Ethiopian farms, work is strictly divided by gender. Men do most of the work in the fields, while women do chores around the house, tend the family's vegetable garden, and help the men with weeding and harvesting. Women are also responsible for buying food, preparing all the meals, and gathering firewood for the cooking stove. Even in the cities, Ethiopian men are usually not involved with the cooking.

Left: **Two Ethiopian children fetch water for the day's cooking.**

Rural Ethiopians produce most of their basic food needs, but they still rely on markets for certain items. About once a week, the woman of the household goes to the local market to buy grain, sugar, spices, meat, and butter. She dries the spices in the sun for several days and then pounds them into a mixture called *berbere* (ber-BERR-ay), which is used to season Ethiopian foods. A simple berbere might contain ginger, cayenne pepper, cinnamon, and cloves. Berbere is the key ingredient that gives wat, or Ethiopian stew, its fiery taste. Another essential cooking ingredient is *niter kebbeh* (NITT-er key-BAY), a mixture of butter, onions, and spices.

Ethiopian bread, or injera, is made from teff flour, which the woman of the house grinds herself. Injera batter is allowed to ferment for three to four days before it is cooked. To make injera, a cook pours a stream of batter onto a hot pan in a circular pattern, allowing the liquid to spread out in a thin layer. In rural areas, women cook injera on a clay griddle over a wood fire; in the city, women usually use a flat pan over a kerosene stove. Injera cooks in a few minutes, forming a soft pancake dotted with air bubbles

Above: **A rural Ethiopian woman prepares the evening meal over an outdoor cooking fire.**

DISHWASHING?

Luckily, Ethiopian women do not have to wash any dishes or silverware. Since Ethiopians eat with their fingers and use injera as a plate, there is nothing left to clean at the end of an Ethiopian meal.

King Solomon and the Queen of Sheba

The legend of King Solomon and the Queen of Sheba is perhaps the most celebrated story in Ethiopia. The Solomonid emperors, Ethiopian Christians, and Ethiopian Jews all have traced their origins to this famous tale, which is also mentioned in the Bible and Islamic literature. In 1955, Ethiopia adopted a new constitution which stated that Emperor Haile Selassie was descended directly "from the dynasty of Menelik I, son of the Queen of Ethiopia, Queen of Sheba, and King Solomon of Jerusalem."

Sheba (known as Makeda to Ethiopians) ruled over what is now Yemen, on the southern Arabian Peninsula. According to legend, Sheba was intrigued by the many stories she heard about King Solomon, who ruled over Israel during the tenth century B.C. Curious to find out how wise Solomon really was, Sheba traveled to Jerusalem. Upon arriving at Solomon's court, she tested the king with a series of riddles. Solomon solved the riddles easily and earned Sheba's respect and loyalty.

Left: **This painting depicts the Queen of Sheba arriving at King Solomon's royal court in Jerusalem.**

In the biblical version of the story, Sheba gave Solomon vast amounts of gold and spices before returning home. In the Ethiopian and Islamic versions, Sheba and Solomon married, and Sheba adopted Solomon's belief in God. Ethiopians believe that Sheba and Solomon had a son, Menelik I, who became the first king of Ethiopia and founder of the Solomonid dynasty, which lasted until 1974. All the Solomonid rulers claimed descent from King Solomon's holy ancestry.

Ethiopian literature also describes the life of the legendary Menelik I. After visiting his father in Jerusalem, Menelik brought the Ark of the Covenant to Ethiopia. The ark, which had been kept in the Temple of Jerusalem, was the chest containing the remains of the Ten Commandments given to Moses by God. When Solomon discovered that Menelik had taken the ark, the Israelite king chased after him with his army. Just as Menelik and his party were about to be captured, they were lifted across the Red Sea into Ethiopia. Ethiopian Christians believe that the ark now rests in St. Mary of Zion Church in Aksum. Scholars have disputed this claim, especially since no one is allowed to see the ark except the priest of the church, but the ark remains an important symbol for Ethiopian Christians.

Above: **The historical city of Aksum contains the ruins of what is believed to be a palace of the Queen of Sheba.**

Peoples of the Southwest

The Southern Nations, Nationalities, and Peoples Regional State is unlike any of the other states in Ethiopia. The population of this southwestern region is split among many small ethnic groups that still pursue ancient lifestyles. Most of these cultures are far removed from modern technology, and they remain isolated by their small communities and the mountainous terrain. Two particularly interesting peoples from this area are the Konso and the Hamer-Banna, who live near the Omo River valley.

The Konso

The Konso are farmers who cultivate their crops on mountainsides. In order to prevent the rain from washing away the soil, the Konso terrace the slopes into large steps, which are about 5 feet (1.5 m) high and 10 feet (3 m) deep. The terraces are supported by stone walls to keep them in place. Common crops include millet, wheat, corn, beans, potatoes, bananas, cotton, and coffee. The complexity of their agriculture has made the Konso a very team-oriented people, with neighbors helping neighbors in the fields.

Above: **The Konso people carve memorial statues to honor dead village members.**

Left: **A pair of Konso women clean cotton, which they will later spin into yarn.**

Most of the Konso live in small, walled villages of up to 3,000 people. The village gates are often decorated with carved wooden statues that honor the dead. Like the Oromo, who practice animist beliefs, the Konso worship a supreme god, whom they believe controls the fertility of their land and animals.

The Hamer-Banna

In the highlands east of the Omo River, a nomadic people called the Hamer-Banna have been living as herders and farmers for centuries. About 20,000 Hamer-Banna live within this patch of Ethiopian savanna, which remains one of the most untouched parts of East Africa. The Hamer-Banna live in temporary camps of thatch-roofed tents, with several families traveling together. Most of the Hamer-Banna are Muslims who incorporate animist beliefs, such as the existence of good and evil spirits, into Islam.

Left: **A Hamer-Banna couple dresses in traditional clothing.**

HAIRSTYLING

Hamer-Banna men are famous for their unique headdresses, which feature a decorated clay cap that indicates one's status or bravery. Young, unmarried Hamer-Banna women often rub fat into their hair, styling it in small curls and coloring it with ocher.

Timkat

Toward the end of the dry season, Ethiopian Christians celebrate Timkat, their most important religious holiday of the year. Timkat is the Ethiopian name for Epiphany, which Christians celebrate twelve days after Christmas. For most Christians, Christmas falls on December 25 and Epiphany on January 6. Ethiopian Christians, however, celebrate Christmas (Ganna) on January 7, which places Timkat on January 19. On Timkat, Ethiopians remember the Magi's discovery of the baby Jesus and his baptism in the Jordan River.

The Procession

On Timkat eve, a priest beats a drum to announce the beginning of the Timkat procession. First, the priests of each church remove the *tabot* (TAH-boht), a model of the Ark of the Covenant, from the inner sanctum where it is kept. A procession emerges from

Left: **A Timkat procession in Addis Ababa displays a rainbow of colors.**

each church with the chief priest leading, followed by another priest carrying the tabot wrapped in an embroidered cloth. Close behind is another row of priests, each wearing colorful robes and carrying fancy umbrellas or metal crosses mounted on staffs. The debtera and altar boys accompany the priests in their slow, solemn march.

Christian villagers quickly join the procession, which stops often for periods of chanting and dancing. At nightfall, the tabot is placed by a pool of water, and the priests guard it throughout the night. At daybreak, worshipers gather at the pool, where one of the elder priests leads a ceremony that reenacts Christ's baptism. After dipping a cross and a burning candle into the pool, the priest sprinkles water over the crowd. When the ceremony is over, the debteras form two long lines and begin to dance. The Timkat procession winds its way back to the village, and everyone goes home to feast. The most spectacular Timkat celebrations take place in Lalibela, where the processions emerge from the famous rock-hewn churches.

Above: **Each of these priests carries a tabot above his head.**

FUN AND GAMES

Ethiopian Christians also celebrate Timkat by playing a special game called guks. Participants dress up in warrior costumes and prepare for a mock battle. Mounted on horseback and armed with wooden lances, opponents charge at each other with blazing speed. Each warrior carries a shield to deflect the lance of his opponent. If a warrior gets knocked off his horse by the opponent's lance, he loses the contest.

74

RELATIONS WITH NORTH AMERICA

Ethiopian relations with Canada and the United States are a relatively recent occurrence in world history, since Ethiopia was cut off from the Western world during most of the eighteenth and nineteenth centuries. Not until Emperor Menelik II's victory at the Battle of Adwa in 1896 did Ethiopia become known as a dominant African power. Ethiopia's firm stance against the Italian invaders at Adwa attracted worldwide attention and left a deep impression on North American leaders.

After World War II, the United States became a close ally of Ethiopia. U.S. military, economic, and humanitarian aid helped keep Emperor Haile Selassie in power during the 1960s and 1970s, despite the civil war with Eritrea. After the fall of the monarchy in 1974, however, Ethiopia became a socialist state with Soviet ties, and U.S. relations suffered.

The tragic Ethiopian famine of 1984 was an emergency call for help. Canadian and U.S. citizens and governments pitched in to donate relief aid and supplies to Ethiopia. Today, the new democratic government of Ethiopia enjoys healthy diplomatic, trade, and cultural relations with North America.

Opposite: **Ethiopian artist Afewerke Tekle created the famous stained glass window that decorates Addis Ababa's Africa Hall, the headquarters for the Organization of African Unity (OAU) and the United Nations Economic Commission for Africa (UNECA). The title of Afewerke's work is "Yesterday's, Today's, and Tomorrow's Africa."**

Left: **Emperor Haile Selassie took part in a parade in New York City during his official visit to the United States on October 5, 1963.**

Building a Strategic Alliance

In 1941, during World War II, Great Britain led the military operation that liberated Ethiopia, Eritrea, and Somalia from Italian rule. Emperor Haile Selassie had cooperated with the British government in the invasion, but he worried about Ethiopian independence as Eritrea and Somalia quickly became part of the British empire. In search of a new ally, Haile Selassie turned to the United States.

Official U.S.-Ethiopian relations had existed since 1903, but they were not of strategic importance until the end of World War II. In 1945, Haile Selassie met with U.S. President Franklin D. Roosevelt to request U.S. support for the annexation of Eritrea to Ethiopia. The Ethiopian government wanted access to the Eritrean coast along the Red Sea, while the U.S. government was interested in establishing a military presence in Mitsiwa and Asmera (both in Eritrea) to observe affairs in Eastern Africa and the Middle East. The United States also saw Ethiopia as a potential supplier of crude oil. In 1949, the Sinclair Oil Corporation, a U.S. petroleum company, landed a fifty-year deal with the Ethiopian government to drill for oil in the Ogaden region.

Below: **Sinclair Oil Field Operations Superintendent Walter J. Wells** *(foreground, left)* **and Ethiopian Emperor Haile Selassie** *(foreground, right)* **presided over the opening ceremony for drilling operations in the Ogaden on May 16, 1949.**

In 1950, the United Nations adopted a plan (fully supported by the United States) to merge Ethiopia and Eritrea in a federation with two separate governments. Carried out in 1952, the federation quickly fell apart. Ethiopia took over Eritrea, and the U.S. government supported Haile Selassie with military and economic aid. In 1963, violence broke out between Ethiopia and Somalia after a Somali rebellion in the Ogaden. When the Soviet Union stepped in as Somalia's new ally, Ethiopia became more dependent on U.S. military support. By 1970, over 2,500 Ethiopian troops had been trained in the United States, and Haile Selassie had received about U.S. $150 million in military aid.

Ethiopia also received U.S. loans and grants to build up its infrastructure, educational facilities, and industries. Ethiopian Airlines, Ethiopia's national airline and one of the renowned airlines of Africa, was founded in 1946 with financial and technical assistance from the United States.

Cultural ties through student exchanges and volunteer organizations also brought Ethiopians and North Americans closer together. Thousands of U.S. and Canadian volunteers worked in Ethiopia with the Peace Corps, a U.S. government agency that provides skilled workers to communities that need social and economic help.

Above: **U.S. military aid provided the Ethiopian army with weapons and training during the 1960s and 1970s. For several years, the U.S. government fully supported Ethiopia during the Eritrean conflict.**

The Alliance Breaks

After Haile Selassie was overthrown in 1974, U.S. officials eagerly waited to see what kind of new government would emerge in Ethiopia. Hopes for a democratic, pro-U.S. leader ended with the rise of Mengistu Haile Mariam. When the socialist Derg regime nationalized all banks, farms, and industries in Ethiopia, the United States demanded compensation for its sizeable investments. Mengistu refused, thus severely damaging U.S.-Ethiopian relations. Human rights abuses and anti-U.S. propaganda by the Derg resulted in the closure of the U.S. communications base in Asmera and the termination of all U.S. military aid to Ethiopia.

In 1977, while Ethiopia was still at war with Eritrea and weakened by the withdrawal of U.S. aid, Somalia invaded the Ogaden. The Derg found a new ally in the Soviet Union, which decided to withdraw its support from Somalia and side with Ethiopia instead. Strengthened by the Soviet alliance, the Ethiopian army promptly forced the Somali invaders to withdraw from the Ogaden in 1978 and nearly defeated the Eritrean secessionists in the north.

Above: **The Derg, led by Chairman Mengistu Haile Mariam** (*pictured in the background, center*), **championed socialism in Ethiopia and struck a military alliance with the Soviet Union in 1977.**

By 1980, U.S.-Ethiopian relations had hit an all-time low. The U.S. Agency for International Development (USAID) terminated its humanitarian aid projects in Ethiopia, and U.S. members of international lending organizations, such as the World Bank, began to vote against loans to Ethiopia. Finally, in July 1980, the Ethiopian government asked the United States to recall its ambassador.

Famine Strikes

Ethiopia had still not recovered from the 1973 famine when an even more devastating hunger crisis struck in the early 1980s. A series of long droughts had crippled Ethiopian agriculture, and various relief agencies called upon foreign governments for emergency aid. Initially, the U.S. government chose not to aid a country aligned with the Soviet Union.

By 1984, the famine had reached disaster proportions. The U.S. government finally realized that, regardless of Ethiopia's political ties, it had to provide help. In 1985, the United States contributed over U.S. $100 million to the relief effort, supplying nearly one-third of Ethiopia's food needs.

Below: **In the early 1980s, prolonged droughts and the civil war with Eritrea resulted in a terrible famine. Rural Ethiopians became refugees, desperate for food and medical care.**

Band Aid and USA for Africa

Around the world, people were concerned about the 1984 famine in Ethiopia. In the United Kingdom, musician Bob Geldof (of the punk band Boomtown Rats) assembled an all-star ensemble of British and Irish pop stars called Band Aid, which recorded the song "Do They Know It's Christmas?" on November 25, 1984. The single, performed by artists such as David Bowie, Boy George, George Michael, Sting, Bono, and Paul McCartney, sold more than 3 million copies worldwide and raised over U.S. $10 million for famine relief in Ethiopia.

In the United States and Canada, major recording artists organized similar groups. In 1985, U.S. entertainer and humanitarian Harry Belafonte founded United Support of Artists for Africa (USA for Africa), a group of musicians committed to helping to resolve crises in Africa. Some fifty pop and rock 'n' roll stars representing USA for Africa teamed up to record the anthem "We Are the World," written by Michael Jackson and Lionel Richie. "We Are the World" went on to become one of the most famous pop songs of all time and generated millions of dollars in aid for Ethiopian and Sudanese famine victims. Another successful hunger relief record was "Tears Are Not Enough" by Northern Lights, a group of Canadian music stars.

Below: **USA for Africa is a humanitarian relief organization that was created by U.S. singer and actor Harry Belafonte. Charity efforts such as USA for Africa and Band Aid have shown that concerned private citizens, not just governments, can make a huge difference in improving the lives of people in need.**

Left: U.S. singer and songwriter Lionel Richie composed the song "We Are the World" with Michael Jackson in 1985.

On July 13, 1985, Geldof united bands and musicians from all over the world in a sixteen-hour benefit concert called Live Aid. Staged simultaneously at Wembley Stadium in London, England, and JFK Stadium in Philadelphia, Pennsylvania, Live Aid featured well-known recording artists such as Madonna, Neil Young, Bob Dylan, Bryan Adams, Elton John, Queen, the Who, Mick Jagger, B. B. King, and Eric Clapton. An estimated 1.4 billion people in over 170 countries saw the concert on television, and more than U.S. $120 million was raised for famine relief.

Above: The 1985 Live Aid concert was a celebration of goodwill and great music. The show raised more money than any single charity event had ever raised.

New Relations with a New Government

In 1991, the Ethiopian People's Revolutionary Democratic Front overthrew the Mengistu regime. The United States quickly recognized Ethiopia's new democratic government and began a new era of economic aid. The U.S. ambassador to Ethiopia returned in 1992, and USAID projects were restarted in 1995. In 1997, Ethiopia received over U.S. $77 million in aid from the United States to further develop agriculture, health care, and education. The Peace Corps returned to Ethiopia in 1994. Besides teaching English, science, and mathematics in Ethiopian schools, Peace Corps volunteers teach communities how to use new technology and how to be more environmentally conscious.

Preserving Stability in Eastern Africa

In 1994, U.S. President Bill Clinton announced the Greater Horn of Africa Initiative, which calls for African governments, relief agencies, and international donors to cooperate in making Eastern Africa more secure in times of famine, poverty, or civil war. One of the main goals of the initiative is to better bridge the distance between relief aid and victims.

In early 1998, Eritrea made territorial claims to northern Ethiopia and then invaded parts of Tigray. Government officials from the United States and Rwanda facilitated talks between Ethiopia and Eritrea in May 1998. The U.S.-Rwanda proposal, which demanded that Eritrean forces withdraw immediately and peacefully from Tigray, was accepted by the Ethiopian government and the Organization of African Unity (OAU); Eritrea rejected the proposal and continued to occupy Ethiopian lands. On June 26, 1998, the United Nations Security Council supported the OAU's framework agreement for a peaceful settlement to the conflict. The Eritrean government later claimed to accept the OAU agreement but still refused to withdraw its troops from Ethiopia. Hostilities resumed on February 6, 1999. After increased fighting in 2000, a cease-fire and a peace treaty were signed.

Above: **President Bill Clinton declared the Greater Horn of Africa Initiative in 1994. Every year, almost 22 million people in Eastern Africa require some kind of outside food aid. The Greater Horn of Africa Initiative is an international effort designed to assist famine-stricken communities and to prevent future hunger crises.**

Ethiopians in the United States

In 1990, the foreign-born population in the United States was about 20 million, with 35,000 of these people born in Ethiopia. Ethiopian immigrants are the third-largest African-born community in the United States, behind Egyptian and Nigerian immigrants. Most Ethiopian immigrants left Ethiopia during the Mengistu regime, leaving behind a country ravaged by civil war, famine, and economic collapse. Today, the Ethiopian immigrant population in the United States is spread out among major cities such as Los Angeles, San Francisco, New York, and Washington, D.C.

Ethiopians living in the United States have had to adjust to differences in climate, food, language, lifestyle, social values, and class structure. Despite the foreign environment, Ethiopian immigrants have become a successful minority group in the United States, forging paths as businessmen, academics, artists, and activists. Some of the most visible Ethiopian immigrants are filmmakers, visual artists, and musicians, who contribute to U.S. culture while spreading awareness about Ethiopian affairs.

EPAN

Ethiopian engineering students founded the Ethiopian Professionals Association Network (EPAN) at the 1999 convention of the National Society of Black Engineers in Kansas City, Missouri. EPAN is a nonprofit organization dedicated to keeping Ethiopian professionals around the world informed and connected.

Left: Haile Gerima is a celebrated Ethiopian-American filmmaker whose works have impressed critics around the world. He often tackles Ethiopian or African-American issues in his films.

Haile Gerima

One of the most famous Ethiopian-American artists is film director Haile Gerima. Born in Gonder in 1946, Gerima came to the United States at the age of twenty-one to study at the Goodman School of Drama in Chicago, where he became interested in filmmaking. He later attended the University of California at Los Angeles (UCLA) and is now a film professor at Howard University in Washington, D.C. His award-winning films include *Harvest 3,000 Years*, which is set in rural Ethiopia, and *Sankofa*, which is a drama about the African slavery experience. In 1999, Gerima finished *Adwa*, a documentary of Ethiopia's victory at the Battle of Adwa in 1896.

Left: Champion Ethiopian runners Abebe Bikila *(leading)* and Mamo Wolde *(behind)* were part of the opening ceremonies for the 1965 World's Fair in New York City.

Cultural Crossroads

Ethiopians and North Americans have developed many different platforms for cultural exchange, including relief organizations, fund-raising charities, academic scholarships, arts and music festivals, business conferences, and sporting events. In 1990, Ethiopians for Peace and Famine Relief staged an important march in Washington, D.C., to draw attention to the situation in Ethiopia. The Canada-Ethiopia Friendship Society, based in Ottawa, Canada, is a nonprofit organization that organizes business ventures, lectures, forums, and aid projects designed to bring Canadians and Ethiopians closer together.

A particularly successful Ethiopian-American organization is the Ethiopian Sports Federation in North America (ESFNA). Founded in 1984 by four sporting clubs from Houston, Dallas, Atlanta, and Washington, D.C., ESFNA now includes more than twenty clubs from major cities in the United States and Canada. Every summer, ESFNA hosts a soccer tournament that rotates among various North American cities. Thousands of Ethiopians from around the world attend the event. Organizers hope that ESFNA will eventually be able to include some traditional Ethiopian games in the tournament.

Rastafarians

Another cultural link between Ethiopia and North America are the Rastafarians, who are part of a back-to-Africa movement that began in the early twentieth century. Rastafarians worship former Ethiopian Emperor Haile Selassie as a divine ruler and believe that Ethiopia is the true homeland of the black race. The name *Rastafarian* comes from Haile Selassie's original name, Ras Tafari. Since the 1950s, the Rastafarian movement has been spread in North America by Jamaican immigrant groups and reggae music. Jamaican reggae artist Bob Marley and his band, the Wailers, were a top international music act of the 1970s that influenced countless North American rock 'n' roll, ska, folk, and reggae groups.

Tourism

Since the EPRDF came into power in 1991, tourism to Ethiopia has been increasing rapidly. In 1998, about 115,000 foreign tourists visited Ethiopia, and the Ethiopian government sees great financial and cultural rewards in further developing the tourism industry. For North American tourists, Ethiopia is a beautiful and ancient country with a fascinating range of local cultures.

Below: **Tourists visit the ruins of a temple in Yeha, Ethiopia's oldest town, located in Tigray. Yeha is over three thousand years old.**

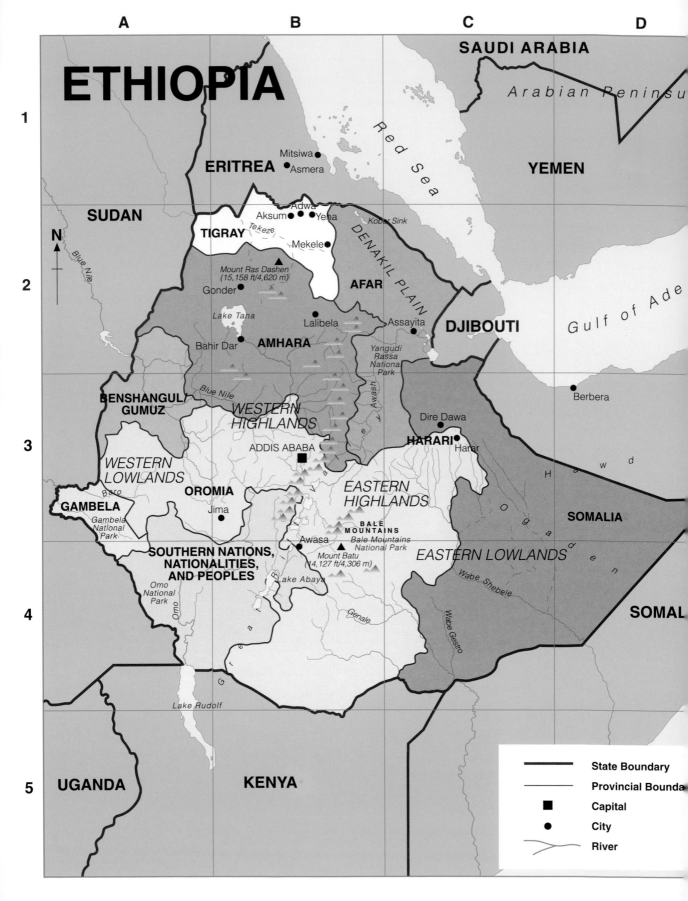

ETHIOPIA

SAUDI ARABIA

Arabian Peninsu

YEMEN

Red Sea

ERITREA

Mitsiwa
Asmera

Adwa
Aksum
Yeha
Kobar Sink

TIGRAY

Tekeze

Mekele

SUDAN

Blue Nile

N

▲ Mount Ras Dashen
(15,158 ft/4,620 m)

Gonder

AFAR

DENAKIL PLAIN

Lalibela

Assayita

DJIBOUTI

Lake Tana

Bahir Dar

AMHARA

Yangudi Rassa National Park

Awash

BENSHANGUL GUMUZ

Blue Nile

WESTERN HIGHLANDS

Dire Dawa

HARARI
Harar

Gulf of Ade

Berbera

WESTERN LOWLANDS

ADDIS ABABA ■

H   w   d

GAMBELA

Baro

OROMIA

Jima

EASTERN HIGHLANDS

SOMALIA

Gambela National Park

BALE MOUNTAINS

Awasa
▲ Mount Batu
(14,127 ft/4,306 m)

Bale Mountains National Park

O   g   a   d   e   n

EASTERN LOWLANDS

SOUTHERN NATIONS, NATIONALITIES, AND PEOPLES

Omo National Park

Omo

Lake Abaya

Genale

Wabe Shebele

Wabe Gestro

G   r   e   a   t

SOMAL

Lake Rudolf

UGANDA

KENYA

━━━	State Boundary
───	Provincial Bounda
■	Capital
●	City
～	River

86

Above: The town of Lalibela is famous for its churches, but even the houses are beautifully constructed.

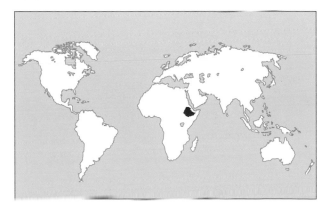

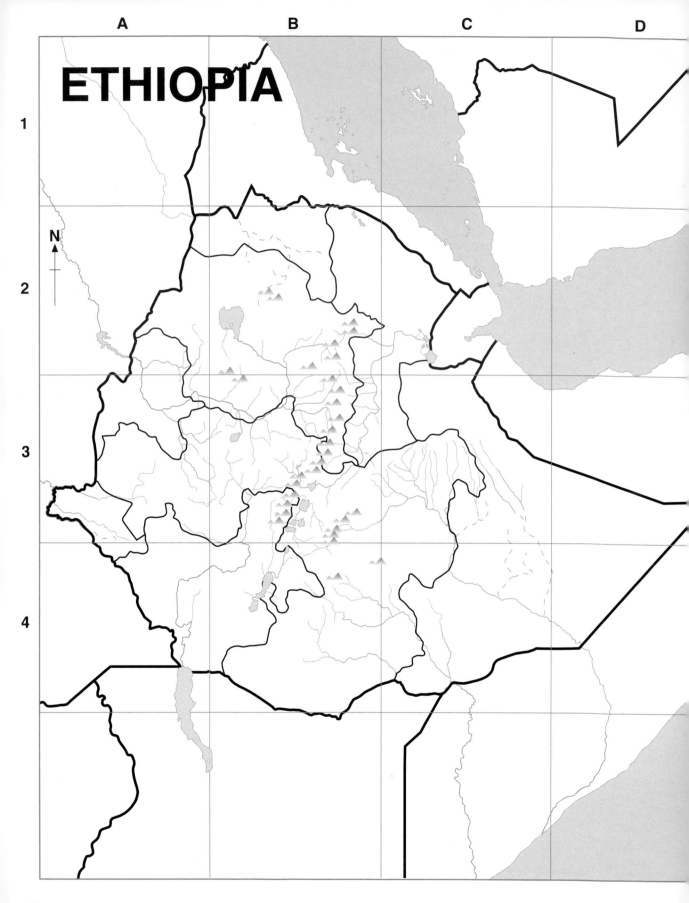

ETHIOPIA

N

A
B
C
D

1
2
3
4

How Is Your Geography?

Learning to identify the main geographical areas and points of a country can be challenging. Although it may seem difficult at first to memorize the locations and spellings of major cities or the names of mountain ranges, rivers, deserts, lakes, and other prominent physical features, the end result of this effort can be very rewarding. Places you previously did not know existed will suddenly come to life when referred to in world news, whether in newspapers, television reports, or other books and reference sources. This knowledge will make you feel a bit closer to the rest of the world, with its fascinating variety of cultures and physical geography.

Used in a classroom setting, the instructor can make duplicates of this map using a copy machine. (PLEASE DO NOT WRITE IN THIS BOOK!) Students can then fill in any requested information on their individual map copies. Used one-on-one, the student can also make copies of the map on a copy machine and use them as a study tool. The student can practice identifying place names and geographical features on his or her own.

Below: **Young Ethiopian shepherds watch over their herd of cattle in the Great Rift Valley.**

Ethiopia at a Glance

Official Name   Federal Democratic Republic of Ethiopia

Capital   Addis Ababa

Official Language   Amharic (official language of the federal government)

Population   70,678,000 (2004 estimate)

Land Area   437,794 square miles (1,134,181 square kilometers)

States   Afar; Amhara; Benshangul/Gumuz; Gambela; Harari; Oromia; Somalia; Southern Nations, Nationalities, and Peoples; Tigray

Highest Point   Mount Ras Dashen 15,158 feet (4,620 meters)

Major Rivers   Awash, Baro, Blue Nile, Genale, Omo, Wabe Shebele, Tekeze

Major Cities   Addis Ababa, Bahir Dar, Dire Dawa, Gonder, Jima, Mekele

Major Languages   Amharic, Arabic, English, Italian, Guraginga, Orominga, Saho, Tigre, Tigrinya, Saho, Sidama, Somali

Head of Government   The prime minister (Meles Zenawi since 1995)

Famous Leaders   Menelik II (1844–1913), Haile Selassie (1891–1975)

Major Religions   Ethiopian Orthodox, Islam, animism, Judaism

Religious Holidays   Christian: Ganna (January 7), Timkat (January 19), Maskal (September 27)

                           Muslim: Eid al-Fitr, Eid al-Adha, Ramadan

Secular Holidays   Victory of Adwa Day (March 2)

                           National Day (May 28)

                           Enkutatash (September 11)

Major Exports   Coffee, leather products, oil seeds, gold

Major Imports   Food products, petroleum, chemicals, machinery

Major Industries   Food processing, beverages, textiles, chemicals, mining

Currency   Birr (8.86 BR = U.S. $1 as of 2003)

Opposite: **A tomb marker stands in an open stretch of the Eastern Lowlands.**

Glossary

Ethiopian Vocabulary

azmari (az-MAH-ree): rural minstrels who sing folk songs.

bega (beh-GAH): the long dry season, lasting from September through February.

belg (BELG): the short rainy season, lasting from March through April.

berbere (ber-BERR-ay): a mixture of spices used to flavor Ethiopian food.

debtera (deb-tuh-RAH): the unordained clergy of the Ethiopian Orthodox Church who perform as musicians and dancers during services and festivals.

demera (dem-uh-RAH): a long pole that is decorated and set on fire during Maskal.

doro wat (DOHR-oh weht): a kind of *wat* containing chicken.

ganna (gehn-NAH): an outdoor Ethiopian sport resembling field hockey.

gebeta (geh-beh-TAH): an African game also known as mancala.

guks (GOOGS): an outdoor Ethiopian sport in which armed horsemen joust.

injera (in-JAYR-ah): a flat, soft, sour bread made from teff flour.

kiremt (ki-REMT): the long rainy season, lasting from June through August.

mesob (meh-SOHB): a large basket used as an eating table.

negus (NEE-gus): the title of king.

niter kebbeh (NITT-er key-BAY): a mixture of butter, onions, garlic, and spices.

tabot (TAH-boht): a box that represents the Ark of the Covenant and is a sacred relic of the Ethiopian Orthodox Church.

tej (TEHJ): a wine made from honey.

tella (TEH-lah): a kind of beer made from barley, corn, or wheat.

wat (WEHT): a spicy meat and vegetable stew eaten with *injera*.

English Vocabulary

abundant: found in great quantities.

accessible: open to use or visitation by a person or persons.

adherents: followers or supporters.

adorned: decorated.

animism: the belief that natural things possess souls.

anthropologists: scientists who study the origins and development of humans.

appendectomy: surgery in which the appendix (a part of the large intestine) is removed from the body.

arable: capable of producing crops.

aromatic: having a strong, fragrant smell.

assimilation: the absorption of a new culture into a group or nation.

autonomous: independent as a self-governing region or nation.

cash-crop farmers: farmers who grow crops that are sold for profit.

communion: a Christian ritual in which worshipers eat bread and drink wine (or grape juice) to remember Jesus's words at the Last Supper.

concentric: having a common center.

cruciform: in the form of a cross.

deforestation: the clearing away of forests to make way for agriculture or industry.

discredited: stripped of a claim or title.

emancipation: the act of freeing or liberating from bondage.

emir: a ruler, chief, or head of state in certain Islamic countries.

endemic: characteristic of a place or area.

federation: union or alliance.

fermented: allowed to sour by using yeast bacteria that break down sugar.

granite: a coarse, volcanic rock.

heir apparent: an heir whose right to the throne cannot be cancelled.

Horn of Africa: the eastern part of Africa made up of Somalia, Djibouti, Eritrea, and Ethiopia.

infrastructure: the facilities, such as roads, communication lines, and power plants, used by the residents of a city or area.

iron oxide: a red-colored compound made up of iron and oxygen.

joust: (n.) a combat in which opponents armed with lances charge each other.

land reforms: programs in which the government redistributes agricultural land among farmers.

lyre: a stringed musical instrument, similar to a harp, that is plucked or bowed.

mismanagement: incompetent or ill-advised regulation.

morality: obedience to a set of laws or rules of conduct.

mortar: a small, thick-walled bowl in which substances are ground into a powder using a pestle.

nationalized: seized by the government for use by the state.

nomads: people who move from place to place without a permanent home.

obelisks: tall, four-sided, stone pillars.

ocher: soil that has an orange-yellow color.

ordained: appointed to a religious office.

pagan: (adj.) not following any of the major world religions.

paraplegic: a person whose legs are paralyzed due to a spinal disease or injury.

pastureland: grassy areas that are suitable for livestock grazing.

persecuted: harassed or oppressed.

pestle: a tool used for grinding or pounding substances in a mortar.

referendum: a vote held to approve a measure or policy.

refugees: people who are forced to flee their homes due to war or crisis.

sanctuaries: areas of land where wild animals are protected from hunters.

sanctum: a sacred or holy place.

savannas: flat plains covered with grass and scattered trees.

seceded: withdrew from a union or alliance.

secessionists: people who wish to separate themselves from a union or alliance.

silt: dirt or sand carried by moving water and deposited downstream.

Somaliland: a historically known coastal area of the Horn of Africa that is now Djibouti and Somalia.

steeps: (v.) soaks in water so as to form a saturated liquid.

subsistence farmers: farmers who raise crops to provide only for the needs of their own families.

suffrage: the right to vote in an election.

teff: a North African grain that is commonly grown in Ethiopia.

tributary: (n.) a stream that flows into a larger stream or other body of water.

welfare: happiness or prosperity.

More Books to Read

Ethiopia. Countries and Cultures series. Allison Lassieur (Bridgestone)

Ethiopia. Cultures of the World series. Steven Gish (Benchmark Books)

The Fire on the Mountain and Other Stories from Ethiopia and Eritrea. Harold Courlander and Wolf Leslau (Henry Holt)

A Glorious Past: Ancient Egypt, Ethiopia, and Nubia. Milestones in Black American History series. Earnestine Jenkins (Chelsea House)

A History of Ethiopia. Harold G. Marcus (University of California Press)

The Lion's Whiskers and Other Ethiopian Tales. Brent K. Ashabranner, editor (Linnet Books)

On the Wings of Eagles: An Ethiopian Child's Story. Jeffrey Schrier (Millbrook Press)

Oromia: An Introduction to the History of the Oromo People. Gadaa Melbaa (Kirk House)

The Return. Sonia Levitin (Fawcett Books)

States of Ethiopia. African Civilizations series. John Peffer (Franklin Watts)

When the World Began: Stories Collected from Ethiopia. Elizabeth Laird (Oxford University Press Children's Books)

Videos

Adwa (Mypheduh Films)

East Africa, Tanzania, and Zanzibar (Lonely Planet)

Globe Trekker: East Africa (555 Productions)

Great Battles of World War II: Europe and North Africa (Ivn Entertainment)

Web Sites

www.cyberethiopia.com

www.ethiopia.nu

www.ethiopia.ottawa.on.ca

www.herald.co.uk/local_info/live_aid.html

Due to the dynamic nature of the Internet, some web sites stay current longer than others. To find additional web sites, use a reliable search engine with one or more of the following keywords to help you locate information on Ethiopia. Keywords: *Addis Ababa, Aksum, Ethiopian Orthodox Church, Falasha, Gonder, Haile Selassie, Harar, Lalibela, Menelik II.*

Index (Note: Ethiopian names are alphabetized according to how they appear in the text.)